LISTEN

LISTEN

CONNECTING TO YOUR
INTUITIVE WISDOM

REB BUXTON

The Flow Farm Press

Contents

This book is dedicated to my mother whose unconditional love, support, and laughs through the years have made my life so beautiful.

listen

Connecting To Your Intuitive Wisdom

ISBN 978-1-7323788-5-8

Design and illustrations by Reb Buxton
Printed in the United States of America
Published by The Flow Farm Press
Nashville, TN
Visit the author's website at www.sacredlife.co

The secret of change is to focus all your energy,
not fighting the old but building the new. - Socrates

The intuitive mind is a sacred gift. - Albert Einstein

A NOTE TO THE READER

This book is for everyone, but much of the tone and language are geared toward men. Why? I am a man and I work with men. If you are a woman, you may be wondering why you should read this book. Let me offer a few suggestions. First, the foundation upon which this book is built is love, wisdom, and integrity. These virtues are worthwhile for anyone, not just men. As a side note, over the years I have found that women seem to be drawn more to the terms compassion, curiosity, and courage. Second, you probably have men in your life and those men need to hear what's in this book. If you read it and recommend it, they are more likely to read it out of respect for you. Third, anecdotally I have observed that men struggle with integrity more than women. If you are a woman and your partner struggles with issues related to integrity, this book could serve as a bridge restoring what has been broken by giving your longing a voice and giving him a path to follow. Finally, this book could also serve as a protection against future lapses in judgment for you and your partner. By committing to live your life by the virtues of love, wisdom, and integrity, you are time traveling to the future and preventing many problems before they occur. Yes, you read that right. By reading and applying what is in this book, you will learn how to time travel.

PART ONE

1

INTUITIVE WISDOM

What is intuitive wisdom and why do you need to connect to it? Intuitive wisdom is a collection of attributes you use every day to make decisions. Intuitive wisdom is not a fixed trait like eye color or height. It is a skill that can be honed like a knife and, when sharpened, used with great precision.

Intuitive wisdom includes various forms of knowledge and understanding combined with the values and virtues needed to live a good life. The physical mechanics of receiving and processing information are logic, emotions, and somatic/body. The three noble virtues are love, wisdom, and integrity. When these six attributes are understood and practiced together as a cohesive unit, they form a powerful foundation to grow your intuitive wisdom.

What problem does intuitive wisdom solve?

Many men have the emotional maturity of a sixteen year old boy. This is not intended to insult but to begin to name the many problems facing men today. The fallout from this epidemic of immaturity is obvious. When a sixteen year old boy acts like a sixteen year old boy we shrug and blame it on youth and immaturity. However, when a grown man with substantially more power acts like a sixteen year old boy it is confusing and problematic.

Are men to blame for this self-inflicted malady? How did we get this way? Has it always been like this or did we devolve to this point? Do men even see the problem?

The reality is that this is a problem hidden in plain sight that the majority of men do not even recognize. I would argue that men are only partially to blame for their failure to mature.

The reason men suffer from arrested development is that no one taught them otherwise. Our fathers came from a generation of men whose primary male stereotype was the rugged individualist who depended on no one and rarely, if ever, showed emotion. Being vulnerable, especially with other men, did not occur because it was considered a sign of weakness and opened you to ridicule and attack.

In certain areas, mostly in urban, more politically and socially liberal areas of the country, change is in the air. Men are realizing they need ceremony, ritual, friends, brotherhood, emotional maturity, sensitivity to the pain men's insecurity and immaturity have caused others but this is the exception not the rule. Men are becoming comfortable in their new roles as stay-at-home dads. Men are going to therapy. Men are seeing the value of deeper relationships with other men.

For eons, men were at the top of the heap when it came to power and control. They made the money. They controlled the money. Women could not get a credit card or open a banking account without their husband's approval until 1975. Now, globalization has moved many blue collar jobs offshore and women have joined the workforce enmasse which has chipped away at the male dominated society. Men are still paid more than women and men control ninety percent of CEO positions at Fortune 500 companies[1] at the time of this writing. However, more than at any time in modern history this landscape is rapidly changing. As women become more and more empowered they no longer need men to be financially secure. Now, they have the ability to choose who they want to date and marry or if they want to marry at all. When it comes to the future of men, Emotional Intelligence is now equivalent to a Harvard degree. Those who have it will succeed. Those who don't will perish.

This brings me to the dark side of being a man in the world today. There is no putting lipstick on this pig. Men, we are in trouble. Here are a few statistics:

- *70% of all suicides in the United States are committed by men*
- *The American Survey Center found that men who have six or more close friends dropped from 55% in 1990 to 27% in 2021*[2]
- *Men with zero close friends grew from 3% in 1990 to 15% in 2021*
- *The Hill reports, "men in their 20's are more likely than women in their 20's to be romantically uninvolved, sexually dormant, friendless and lonely"*[3]
- *People who experienced social isolation had a 32% higher risk of dying early from any cause compared with those who weren't socially isolated. Participants who reported feeling lonely were 14% more likely to die early than those who did not.*[4]

These are a small sample of the troubling trends facing men today. Men are struggling and fewer men have relationships with men or women to help them navigate the choppy waters of being a man in America.

The multitude of reasons why men hit an emotional ceiling as teenagers are significant and preventable. Let's begin with a phenomenon called *group mind*. Researchers have been baffled by human behavior in crowds. People tend to do things in groups they would never do individually. If a man is in a group of men and is more mature, well-spoken, and emotionally intelligent he isn't going to get a slap on the back with an atta-boy for his good work. He is a threat and men have one way of dealing with threats and that is violence. It becomes a matter of survival for most men to just get in line with the rest of the men and tolerate, or even perpetuate, bad behavior. We are a pack species and people don't survive in a pack by standing out from the pack. Historically, men have not been a safe place for men.

Another reason men fail to advance in emotional maturity is that they don't need to be more mature to find a romantic partner. This dynamic is changing as women are more in control of their destiny but it still holds true for the majority.

If a woman is looking at the dating pool and sees that most men are relatively the same when it comes to emotional maturity, it is easy to lose hope of finding their emotional equal and elevate other important factors such as attraction, ability to financially sustain themselves, and the feeling of safety (or lack thereof) they feel around a particular man.

In some sense, it is like the world went and changed but men never got the memo. This conundrum brings us back to the question, "What problem does intuitive wisdom solve?"

The objective of this book is to help men grow in emotional intelligence by teaching them how to listen to themselves and love themselves. People who love themselves don't kill themselves. People who learn to listen to themselves are skilled at finding solutions to life's many problems and are more likely to make the world a better place not worse.

What men need to overcome these obstacles is a plan. If you want to motivate a man, give him a purpose, point him in a direction, and show him how to use the best tools to get the job done. Something heroic will emerge. When a man sees his life as having meaning he is destined for greatness.

Most men long to be a hero even if it is just to his wife, his partner, his kids, his family and friends. Greatness is woven into the DNA of every man but along with that greatness there is a problem of epic proportions.

People are irrationally afraid of what I call "Out There" evil. "Out There" evil is the stuff of Hollywood blockbusters like *The Exorcist* or *The Silence Of The Lambs*. We believe "Out There" evil is lurking in the bushes or it's the serial killer roaming the streets at night. "Out There" evil seems to be everywhere but it's nebulous and beyond our control. However, it isn't the "Out There" evil that causes so many of our problems. We should be far more concerned about what I call "In Here" evil.

Woven inextricably into the fabric of every human heart is the capacity for great love and great evil. They coexist together. We are all infected with the virus of evil. "In Here" evil is the only evil you need to be worried about because it is the only evil you have the power to control. You control your capacity to commit evil acts by shunning greed, jealousy, and anger and instead focusing your energy on being a loving individual.

We live in a broken, fragile world that needs more heroes and less villains. You can be a hero by committing to live your life by the virtues of love, wisdom, and integrity. This is also the strongest weapon against your own "In Here" evil.

The potential for great evil and great good that exist within us all are forever jockeying for your energy and attention. The quality of your life will be solely determined on which one you chose to follow. Do you give into your darker, selfish impulses or your more noble, virtuous aspirations? The choice is *always* yours.

This epic battle between good and evil is not a black and white dichotomy. We all make bad choices and do things we regret. We are not perfect. The difference though is how we respond when we make mistakes. A heart oriented toward love will respond radically different than a heart oriented toward evil.

The biggest obstacle to a man being great is being unaware of the game he's playing. If a man doesn't realize he has the emotional maturity of a sixteen year old boy he is going to be handicapped because he isn't pursuing a solution because he doesn't see the problem. If a man inherits racist or sexist beliefs from his family and community and lacks awareness, he will perpetuate those beliefs and nurture the evil in his heart.

By naming these roadblocks to a man's maturity, I am not attempting to relieve men of the responsibility for who they have become. Every man is responsible for himself. No excuses. It is hard in today's electronically connected world to claim ignorance of the role men's deficiencies play in the breakdown of our society.

These are the problems. What are the answers?

One answer to these and many other societal maladies is surprisingly simple. But as with many things, simple does not mean easy. The good news is that men don't require the solutions to be easy to accomplish great things. Men know how to work hard to complete a difficult task.

The simple solution to these complex problems comes down to two sentences:

You must keep doing the work because the work never ends. The work is to grow in love, wisdom, and integrity and to help others grow in love, wisdom, and integrity.

It is my deep desire and mission in life to help men learn how to live each day with love, wisdom, and integrity. These eternal virtues will empower you to live courageous lives. They will protect you from unnecessary harm. They will protect those you love most in this world. They will ensure your success. They will guide you through difficulties and hardships. They will provide you with a deep and abiding sense of inner peace.

I call this type of living *The Sacred Life*. Once you commit to living each day with love, wisdom, and integrity life becomes much easier. Life actually becomes more joyful because your personal demons fade into the background and your better angels step forward. You don't struggle with the right thing to do like you did in the past because you have a plan when life gets hard and confusing. You also have a plan of what to do when things are great!

Many men are very loving individuals. Many men possess a great deal of wisdom. Where a significant number of men stumble is with integrity. I felt the definition of integrity needed a refresh so I came up with my own. Integrity is holding yourself accountable to your own greatness. A simpler way to think about integrity is having the courage to do the next right thing. How do you know what the next right thing is in any given situation? This brings us back to the beginning and intuitive wisdom.

Let's review. Intuitive wisdom includes various forms of knowledge and understanding combined with the values and virtues needed to live a good life. The physical mechanics of receiving and processing information are logic, emotions, and somatic/body. The three noble virtues are love, wisdom, and integrity. When these six attributes are understood and practiced together as a cohesive unit, they form a powerful foundation to grow your intuitive wisdom.

In this book you will learn how to harness the power of your mind, your emotions, and connect to your body. You will learn *The Transformational Path*, a process for how to solve any problem. You will learn how to connect with yourself everyday in what I call *Sacred Space*. You will also learn how to love yourself. You will use all of these new skills to climb your *Sacred Mountains*.

Here is a blessing I speak over myself every day and I want to do the same for you as we begin this journey together:

May you be loving today
May you seek wisdom today
May you act with integrity today
May you have a courageous heart today

2

SELF-IMPROVEMENT ADDICT

Hi, my name is Reb! I am a self-improvement addict. What makes me a self-improvement addict? I can't resist the urge to consume books, podcasts, magazines, news articles, self-help websites, research papers, retreats, social media reels, mobile apps, anything about psychology, the mind, personal growth, neuroscience, optimizing performance, spirituality, or any topic even tangentially related to becoming a better person.

Here is an example of my addiction in real life. Some time ago while on one of my listening walks, a question popped into my mind that changed the course of my life. The question was, "What happens when we die?" Growing up in a devoutly religious home, I attended more than my fair share of religious events including Sunday morning services, Sunday night services, Wednesday night services, revivals, Christian summer camps, and weekly youth groups to name just a few. I was so indoctrinated into the conservative Christian mindset that I believed I knew the answer to this question. But I chose to listen to myself and followed my instinct to explore the idea. One thing led to another, and over the course of a year I read nearly 80 books on death, dying, near-death experiences, and life after death. I had many fascinating experiences that took me to some wild, wonderful, and strange places, altering and reshaping my beliefs about what happens when we die.

When it comes to my addiction, my drug of choice is information. Like any good obsession, it takes more and more information to get the same high of enlightenment. I can enhance these experiences by listening to a book or podcast while exercising.

If you are reading this book, you may be like me. Are you always on the lookout for the next fix that will "level up your game," "help you reach 20x your potential," or "how to live your most amazing life"?

I have a confession. I chose the subtitle of this book because I knew no self-respecting self-improvement addict could resist finding out the secrets to connecting to their intuitive wisdom. That would be like a hungry fish swimming away from a shiny lure. Ain't gonna happen. Please forgive me for manipulating the ventral tegmental area of your brain. I'm just a guy trying to make a dollar to feed his kids.

Let me ask you a question. How many personal development books and podcasts did you consume in the past twelve months? Ten? Twenty? Fifty? A hundred?

Let me ask you another question. Once you listened to each podcast or read each book, how much time did you spend reviewing the material to understand how to apply it to your life? How deep of a dive did you take into studying and doing the work prescribed? If you are anything like me, not much. Why? Because we're addicts!

As soon as I finish consuming information, I move on to the next new discovery, system, modality, or treatment that will rescue me from that lazy procrastinator in my brain. If you are like me, you probably have a long list of books waiting for you at the library, more queued up on your phone, and half a dozen on your nightstand. My insatiable consumption is similar to frat boys' shotgunning beers on Spring Break in Panama City Beach.

Calling us addicts is good for a laugh, but behind the humor, our behavior has a serious flaw. Why are we so addicted to information that makes us better, smarter, and more efficient yet fail to spend time truly implementing what we are learning? Why do we roam from one self-improvement fad to the next, like cattle grazing in a pasture, moving from one tuft of grass to another without applying the valuable information?

I am not addicted to books and podcasts as much as I am addicted to learning. It started in college when I first experienced the power of reading. Growing up in rural Mississippi in the 1980s, I never read a book in high school. Not. A. Single. Book.

Back then, audiobooks were on cassette tapes and the internet was not a thing. If you wanted to read a book, you went to the bookstore or a local library where the Dewey Decimal System awaited you on paper index cards.

After reading my first book in college, something in my brain turned on like a light in a dark room. It was only a John Grisham novel, but I was hooked and more than a little curious about what I had been missing by not reading. It wasn't long before I was diving into Stephen Hawking's *A Brief History Of Time*, Douglas Hofstadter's *Gödel, Esher, Bach: An Eternal Golden Braid,* and Joseph Campbell's *The Power Of Myth.*

I realize now that a curious mind is a creative machine capable of adapting and problem-solving at the highest levels. Once the mind expands, it cannot return to its former shape.

Most authors of self-improvement books are fine folks who have done a lot of soul-searching and personal development themselves. They have paid their dues and learned their lessons through trial and error. In a well-intentioned effort to help people, they put pen to paper (or fingers to keyboard), reducing their ideas into bite-sized nuggets of wisdom easily consumed by the masses.

Authors practically spoon-feed us what took them decades of trial and error to assimilate. It is presumptuous of us to think we can grasp that level of complexity and nuance without putting in the hard work necessary to learn it. We become like the rock skipping across the top of a lake when we need to slow down and sink to the bottom. We move effortlessly from book to book and podcast to podcast, believing we are more intelligent. In our frenzy, we don't allow the information to create any real change. In other words, we don't learn the wisdom because we don't earn the wisdom.

There are no shortcuts to being great at anything. If you want to excel, you must put in the time, pay attention, make mistakes, and learn the lessons. I, too, will spoon-feed you information, but only after helping you acknowledge your addiction and become your own self-improvement guru by teaching you to listen to yourself.

One of the most effective ways to learn how to listen to yourself is by developing a daily *Personal Listening Practice* that I call *Sacred Space*. You can make this time to be whatever you want but one effective method for listening to yourself is some form of journaling. I can hear collective groans from the tens of people reading this book, "Oh no! I'll do anything but journal! Please no! The horror!"

People think they hate journaling because they can't write, don't have time, aren't morning people, don't write beautiful prose, have ADHD and can't sit still for very long, or their hand cramps up when they write (yes, one client attempted to escape journaling using this excuse).

The real reason why people hate journaling is that it's hard work and doesn't provide instant gratification like a dopamine shot from social media, the burn of a yoga class, or the fun-filled frolic of a Smartless podcast. It's just you, a pen, a journal, and a lot of silence. You didn't think you could get away with journaling on a computer, did you?

Why is journaling so important? Journaling is honest, hard work. It combines listening to yourself, trusting yourself, and loving your-self all mixed together. It is also about getting practical answers to your most pressing questions. Journaling will help you clarify and then achieve what you most desire. Do you see the central character in each category? You. You! & YOU!!

Journaling prepares you for making decisions. The more you con-nect with your intuitive wisdom, the more benefit you will gain from trusting yourself. Over time, you develop unshakable confidence and that elusive inner peace from feeling safe with yourself.

The heart of any great romantic relationship, the satisfaction of being a great parent, the courage to overcome addictions, the power to heal after a tragedy, and finding inner peace in a chaotic world are all built on loving yourself.

Journaling is a way to tap into the power of your intuitive wisdom. That doesn't mean you don't seek support from other wise souls who have walked the path before you. It would be foolish not to learn from M. Scott Peck, Bessel van der Kolk, Brene Brown, Irvin Yalom, Don Miguel Ruiz, Maya Angelou, Paulo Coelho, Stephen Covey, or Victor Frankl. The lessons these masters teach are profound.

The warning bell I am ringing is this: do not get so caught up in just plowing through one book after another and deceiving yourself that somehow the information will be absorbed simply because you heard it once. Seek the wisdom you already possess, then search out experts in what you want to learn, but take your time and go slow. There is a reason the best-tasting barbeque takes so long to cook.

Slowing down requires willpower. To be thoughtful about how you digest information takes discipline. A change may be needed. Instead of thirty books a year, read twenty. Out of those twenty pick out three that truly inspire you and reread each book two or three times in quick succession.

In my line of work, I come across lots of self-help books. Even with my new filters, I cannot resist a great title with an elegant, eye-catching cover. I have reigned myself in but still listen to several books a month. Here is one strategy I use to overcome my self-improvement addiction.

If I am halfway through a book and do not feel inspired, I don't continue reading it. There are better ways to spend the minutes of my life. I once thought I needed to finish every book I started, not doing so felt like a character flaw. Now, not so much. If I do finish a book and don't find it helpful, I quickly move on.

However, if a book profoundly impacts me, I purchase it in the opposite format I read it. If I listened to the book, I buy a physical copy.

When I experience the material differently, I process the information as if hearing it for the first time. This helps reinforce the salient points. As I reread each book, I pay close attention to what stands out, jotting down notes in my journal, or bookmarking parts of the audiobook for later review.

I am constantly amazed at how much critical information I missed in the first reading. Rereading (or relistening) allows me to slow down, take notes, and put the wisdom into practice. I can visit the author's website for additional resources, find other books they have written, watch interviews of them on YouTube, or attend one of their events. I can only do this with about three or four books a year, but I am taking the time to learn the wisdom by earning the wisdom.

The message I want you to take from this book is this: If you love yourself, every self-help book, therapeutic modality, problem-solving skill, self-improvement podcast, weekend workshop, and week-long retreat will work. If you don't love yourself, none of them will work. Loving yourself is your most important job. I call it a job because loving yourself takes work. By slowing down and consuming less, you will have less self-help in your life but more help yourself.

3

LISTEN

Your inner life is a sacred place. It is your private sanctuary where you and you alone ponder, dream, and create your life. It is the birthplace of decisions that become actions that become your destiny.

Your mind is a busy place. On any given day, it is bombarded with a steady stream of sensory information and requests for your time, attention, and money. It seems everything and everyone wants a piece of your mental real estate.

Due to this relentless assault, you are not responsible for what comes into your mind. You are only responsible for what you allow to linger there because what you think about you become. This point is made abundantly clear in Ethan Kross' book *Chatter* where he writes:

A study published in 2010...found that inner experiences consistently dwarf outer ones. What participants were thinking about turned out to be a better predictor of their happiness than what they were actually doing. This speaks to a sour experience many people have had: You're in a situation in which you should be happy (spending time with friends, say, or celebrating an accomplishment), but a ruminative thought swallows your mind. Your mood is defined not by what you did but by what you thought about.

The mental and physical energy you expend reflects what you most value and becomes an expression of your personal power. Your power is a precious, limited commodity and should be treated as such. Wherever you allow your thoughts to go, your energy (and power) will flow.

If you marginalize the process of choosing how and where you give away your power, you will embolden others to take advantage of you. Situations in which an imbalance of power exists will break you down rather than build you up. Operate in this state for too long and you will become mentally and physically ill. You will remain sick until you bring your body back into balance, reclaim your power, and foster inner peace.

What you allow yourself to think about is important, but equally important is how you think about what you think about. You get to choose both the subject and the quality of your thoughts. This proactive approach to your mental health and wellness will inevitably manifest an exceptional life.

What does it mean to connect to your intuitive wisdom? How do you do it? Why is it so important? In this book you will learn how to listen to yourself and love yourself in a more mature, sustainable manner. You will learn methods to solve problems and create a more fulfilling life. You will come to understand how the whispers of your deepest thoughts are the doorway to your most profound insights.

You will also learn how to connect to your heart, mind, and body to bring depth, nuance, creativity, wonder, and awe into your life. When you bridge the chasm between your heart, mind, and body you create a unified self. This whole person is the optimal state for solving life's most perplexing problems and living an amazing life.

Life often feels chaotic and lacks a cohesive narrative from moment-to-moment. Only after the fact does life make a little more sense. However, you are responsible for creating a meaningful story from the fragments of your experiences. How you think about your life experiences is critical for creating a positive, hopeful storyline.

You listen to yourself every day, all day. When you make time to listen to yourself with love, wisdom, and integrity, you are creating a *Sacred Space*. This shift toward love, wisdom, and integrity will guide you out of the Valley of Despair and up the steep slopes to the peaks of your Sacred Mountains.

There is no limit on the amount of love you can give yourself and no substitute for this exercise but you must practice. The more you practice, the better you become at taking care of yourself and eliminating threats to your mental, physical, emotional and spiritual health.

You will learn a step-by-step process for prioritizing a *Sacred Space* in your daily schedule. You will learn how to listen to yourself in a more profound, loving, courageous manner. As you listen to yourself with love, wisdom, and integrity, you come to trust yourself. This new trusting relationship will help you feel safe with yourself. From this safe, trusting place, loving yourself naturally flows. You gain the clarity and confidence to create your best life in this new loving flow state.

To truly love someone else, you must love yourself because you cannot love anyone more than you love yourself. When you listen to yourself, you will always have a friend. When you love yourself, you will never be alone.

4

INNER PEACE

What is it that you most desire? Did something immediately come to mind or are you unsure what you want? What I have found that everyone is seeking, whether they realize it or not, is inner peace. Everything we do is an attempt to find inner peace.

Inner peace is ideal for solving problems, improving relationships, making better decisions, and living a vibrant life. There are many ways to cultivate inner peace. No one way is superior to another. If everybody is searching for inner peace, why do so few people have it?

In 1980, John Travolta starred in the award-winning film *Urban Cowboy.* One of the songs on the soundtrack was Johnny Lee's *Looking For Love.* It is a toe-tapping little ditty with a catchy chorus:

I was lookin' for love in all the wrong places
Lookin' for love in too many faces

If I were to rewrite these lyrics to fit the theme of this book, it might sound something like this:

I was lookin' for peace in all the wrong places
Lookin' for peace in too many faces

We keep looking for peace in all the wrong places. We look for it in relationships. We look for it in divorces. We look for it in money and we look for it in all the things money can buy. What most people don't do is look for it within themselves.

Looking inward and not outward is the surest path to finding authentic, lasting inner peace. Learning to listen to yourself and love yourself are two ways to do the inner work necessary to find that elusive inner peace.

The primary reason most people don't listen to themselves is because they don't know how. No one ever taught them the power of listening to their intuitive wisdom. Every day, you hear that chattering voice in your head, but rarely do you think to engage it, reshape it, or transform it. With guidance, you can turn that chatter into a voice of wisdom helping you discover and achieve what you most desire.

As your listening skills develop, opportunities for loving yourself will naturally manifest all around you. As you intentionally choose to love yourself, you bridge the divide between your heart, mind, and body healing yourself.

Another reason people fail to listen to themselves is that they have lost trust in themselves to make good decisions because their past is littered with regrettable choices. While this is a formidable obstacle, there is a path forward.

What will you do with the long list of poor decisions in your past? You may be the kind of person who typically makes good decisions, but you have occasionally strayed from your values causing a series of unfortunate events. How do you forgive yourself and move forward?

In my work over the past twenty years, I have concluded that truth is simple, always good, and never changes. The answer to how you free yourself from guilt and shame and start making good decisions after making some bad ones comes down to three words. As we discussed, overcoming your self-doubt means creating a better version of yourself by committing to live each day according to love, wisdom, and integrity.

No one would dispute the nobility of love, wisdom, and integrity. However, many people need guidance in applying them to their daily lives. Each of the three virtues has a corresponding path to achieve that specific virtue. For love, the path is compassion. For wisdom, the path is curiosity. For integrity, the path is courage.

To be loving is to cultivate compassion for yourself first and then others. It is common knowledge that metaphorically you can't run before you walk and you can't walk before you crawl. Some things must come before others. To love others, you must first love yourself. You cannot love others more than you love yourself and having compassion for yourself is the foundation of achieving what you most desire.

Love is the greatest of all virtues and stands head and shoulders above everything else. All forms of compassion are love in action. St. Paul spoke to the power of love by telling his friends, "*If I speak with human eloquence and angelic ecstasy but don't love, I'm nothing but the creaking of a rusty gate. If I give everything I own to the poor but I don't love, I've gotten nowhere. So, no matter what I say, what I believe, and what I do, I am bankrupt without love[5].*"

Wisdom comes from curiosity about yourself, others, and the world, but that isn't the only way to earn wisdom. I once heard someone say that wisdom is what you get when you don't get what you want.

If love is king, then curiosity is queen. Someone who is not curious about themselves, others, and life is a dull blade useful to no one. A curious mind is insatiable, always searching for answers. Wisdom gained from curiosity will help you avoid many unfortunate events and a lot of unnecessary suffering.

Knowing the right thing to do requires wisdom, but bringing that noble idea to life often requires courage, especially when that action costs you something. What you do during those moments of being tested will depend on how well you prepared before that moment arrived.

I can trace every poor decision, bad outcome, and persistent problem I have had to a lack of love, wisdom, and integrity. I wavered and made decisions that satisfied my ego when I needed to be courageous and sacrificed what I wanted for the greater good.

I failed to have integrity at critical moments because I had no code to live by. Instead, I made decisions based on emotions. Emotions are great allies but terrible leaders. They reveal what we care about but often lead to self-centered reactions.

Whether you realize it or not, you live by a code. Your life is defined by what you do and what you do is determined by your beliefs. What you believe becomes your code. The default code most people accept without question is some combination of the influence of their friends and family, the greater society and culture, and their community's political/religious norms.

Societies worldwide have attempted to embed a higher moral code in their citizens. One example is the military. Another example is marriage. Take wedding vows. How many people have recited the words for richer or poor, in sickness and health, till death do us part? Did they take time to consider the implications of their commitment? Probably not. Who does? If wedding vows don't offer protection from infidelity and direction when your relationship struggles, what good are they?

The virtues of love, wisdom, and integrity and their corresponding pathways of compassion, curiosity, and courage are a code you can choose. They will prevent many problems from ever occurring. They are helpful when life throws you a curveball that doesn't break and hits you in the head at ninety miles an hour.

When the virtues of love, wisdom, and integrity become your North Star, you can confidently trust that your decisions have a solid foundation. Even if it all goes to hell, you will have inner peace. You will no longer be dependent on good outcomes for your happiness. If good things happen to you, that's fantastic. Celebrate your success! However, outcomes are almost always beyond your control due to factors beyond your reach. Acting with love, wisdom, and integrity will never let you down because they are absolutely in your control all the time.

Nothing is more powerful than the synergy of love, wisdom, and integrity. Each virtue needs the other two to reach their fullest expression. Love without wisdom and integrity is reckless. Wisdom without love and integrity is aimless. Integrity without love and wisdom is harsh and rigid. They all need each other to form a harmonizing balance. To hear a magnificent example of the power of harmony and balance, search YouTube for *The Ecclesium Choir* singing *Lully, Lulla, Lullay*[6]. Take a moment to bring up the song and listen as you finish reading this chapter. It will be the perfect accompaniment and maybe the most beautiful four minutes of your day.

In this book, there is a lot of emphasis on you, the individual. However, as we begin it is good to pause and remember that you are not alone. There are forces far greater than ourselves at work in the world though to believe this requires an element of faith. To put this mystery into perspective I googled "largest known object in the universe" and came across the *Hercules-Corona Borealis Great Wall*[7]. It is a supercluster of galaxies that would take ten billion years to travel from one side to the other if you were traveling at the speed of light which is 186,000 miles per second. The incredible size of the universe is a reminder to stay humble and admit there may be things we do not know or fully understand.

You must remind yourself to keep doing the work because the work never ends. The work is to grow in love, wisdom, and integrity and help others grow in love, wisdom, and integrity.

As small as you and I are in this big universe, you are not insignificant. It might be helpful to think of your life like this. The decisions you make today matter a great deal. They will follow you for all eternity.

5

CONNECTING TO YOUR HEART

As you learn to listen to and love yourself, learning how to connect to your heart will be a vitally important tool to guide you in cultivating both pursuits. Connecting to your heart may sound like a sentimental gesture. If that language is too flowery for you, a more practical definition would be bringing attention to the center of your chest. It is literally that simple.

Advances in science and technology have revealed how the heart is more than just a pump. At the forefront of this research is the Heartmath Institute. Founded in 1991 by Doc Childre, this nonprofit's vision is to create "A kinder, heart-centered world where we care for one another and live harmoniously in peace."

In their publication *Science of the Heart*, Rolin McCraty, Ph.D. states: *New research shows the human heart is much more than an efficient pump that sustains life. Our research suggests the heart also is an access point to a source of wisdom and intelligence that we can call upon to live our lives with more balance, greater creativity and enhanced intuitive capacities. All of these are important for increasing personal effectiveness, improving health and relationships and achieving greater fulfillment.*

31

We live in a society that celebrates left-brain, logic-based, rational thinking while tolerating emotions. This is out of balance with the optimal performance of a mind, heart, and body-based system. The purpose of connecting to your heart is to build a bridge between your emotional intelligence and your intellect, where signals freely travel back and forth. Why is this bridge so vital?

Thinking and feeling are not the same thing. Thinking about loving someone is not the same as feeling love for a real person and committing to them for the rest of your life. Thinking and feeling have two very different functions but serve the same mission. The mission is to unite the mind, body, and heart so they operate as efficiently and effectively as possible to keep you safe and help you perform at a high level to be successful in a competitive world.

The neurobiology of the heart-brain connection is complex and dynamic and much too complicated to detail in a single chapter[8]. The short version of the story is that from the inception of modern medicine, the brain was thought to control the heart. However, researchers in the field of neurocardiology (which was formed from the collective fields of cardiology, neurophysiology, and neuroanatomy) concluded that the heart is replete with neurons just like those in the brain. These neurons allow the heart to function independently and form a "little brain" called the *heart-brain*[9].

The discovery that the heart had neurons eventually led to more revelations. Not only does the heart send signals to the brain, but other organ systems communicate with the brain in the same way. This communication is called interoception.

Researchers and practitioners have shown an increased interest in interoception because of its practical application to help treat common ailments such as anxiety and depression. Those with greater sensitivity to interoceptive signals can better regulate emotions and self-regulate internal states. David Robson writes, "It is only by listening to the heart, it seems, that we can take better care of the mind."[10]

Most of the body's functions happen beyond conscious awareness on the subconscious plane. Only a small portion of those signals ever rise to a level of conscious perception. One example of signals you can perceive is the rhythmic beating of your heart. It is common for many people to struggle to perceive their beating heart, yet the sensitivity to this function (interoception) proves to be most helpful.

Those suffering from depression find it more difficult to connect to their hearts than non-depressed individuals. Conversely, those who suffer from anxiety exacerbate their reactions to even the slightest increase in heart rate. This results in an exaggerated response to a minor situation, which leads to a greater stress response and panic.

We live in an stress-drenched society. We compare ourselves to our friends on social media. We helplessly watch those suffering around the world on the news. It is no secret that stress increases the likelihood of disease. McCraty continues: *Unspecified negative emotional arousal, often described as stress, distress or upset, has been associated with a variety of pathological conditions, including hypertension, silent myocardial ischemia, sudden cardiac death, coronary disease, cardiac arrhythmia, sleep disorders, metabolic syndrome, diabetes, neurodegenerative diseases, fatigue and many other disorders. Stress and negative emotions have been shown to increase disease severity and worsen prognosis for individuals suffering from a number of different pathologies. On the other hand, positive emotions and effective emotion self-regulation skills have been shown to prolong health and significantly reduce premature mortality. From a psychophysiological perspective, emotions are central to the experience of stress[11].*

To round out our understanding of the importance of connecting to your heart, we need to discuss Heart Rate Variability, most commonly referred to as HRV.

HRV refers to the fluctuations, or variability, between each heartbeat, not the heartbeat itself. A greater degree of variability is generally considered good because it shows the body's ability to adapt to different situations. A low HRV indicates potentially current and even future health problems.

As early as 1965, scientists knew the importance of monitoring HRV. It was observed that during labor, fetal distress (a sign that the baby is not doing well) was preceded by decreased HRV before any changes in the baby's heart rate were detected. In people with diabetes, lower HRV predicted nerve damage before any symptoms appeared.

Until the epic leap in technology regarding mobile phone devices in the early 2000s, only research facilities at hospitals and universities had access to the machines sensitive enough to measure heart rate variability and heart coherence. Now, anyone can hack into their nervous system, brain waves, and heart-brain for a few hundred dollars. Devices such as the Aura Ring, Apple Watch, Muse Headband, or Heartmath monitor and their accompanying apps will answer definitely in real time if you are meditating correctly while also monitoring your heart rate variability.

Over the years, I have convinced many people to try meditation because meditation has many proven health benefits. Some of those benefits include reduced stress, improved memory, better sleep, lower blood pressure, and more compassion. However, most people quit soon after they began. The reason most cited for ending their practice was uncertainty around whether or not they were doing it right.

Meditating is one of the best ways to listen to your body, your emotions, and your mind. Nothing will amplify the noise between your ears to reveal what you need to work on more than sitting quietly in a room alone for an extended period of time. The best way to avoid the pitfall of not knowing if you are meditating correctly is to use a device that gives instant feedback. I prefer the Muse App and headband, but they are all good in their own way.

Here is how Muse works. The Muse headband and similar technologies measure and map brain waves, pulse, and skin conductivity. When you change your state and relax your mind, your brain waves shift from beta and gamma to alpha, theta, and delta.

The Muse headband and app have audio and visual feedback features, letting you know in real time when you are switching from high-energy brain waves to more relaxed signals. After the meditation session, the app visually illustrates each brain wave into a graph that categorizes your session into three categories: calm, neutral, or active. It shows the percentage of time spent in each category. Two other graphs display how still or active you were and your average pulse rate[12].

In the Mind section of the Muse app, you get to select from a variety of soundscapes including a bustling city, a campfire, a rushing river, the ocean waves crashing on the shore, a rainstorm, or desert winds.

If you are distracted and unfocused when you begin meditating, the noises get louder and more chaotic. This indicates you are in more active brain wave patterns. When you connect to your heart by focusing on the center of your chest, the sounds calm down and fade into the background. When you stay relaxed for five seconds or longer, birds start chirping, letting you know you are maintaining an optimal state.

Technology has made connecting to your heart easy. As you learn to connect with your heart using your preferred device and smartphone app, you will be more confident about connecting to your heart without the device when you are at work, on a date, playing sports, or with family during the holidays. You can engage in interoceptive practices that help you maintain awareness and moderate your reaction to stressful situations. Connecting to your heart may be one of the easiest and most valuable skills you learn in this book.

A simple way to connect to your heart is a practice I created called *The Three Slow Breaths* exercise. To begin, pause and bring your attention to your chest by placing the palm of your left hand over your heart. Feel the warmth of your hand and the slight rising and falling of your chest as you breathe. Close your eyes and take a normal breath in and a normal breath out. Next, slow down your breath slightly and breathe in and out again. Finally, take one more breath in a little slower than the last breath and breathe out a little slower. Open your eyes and you're done. Closing your eyes is optional but I find it helpful to concentrate. It is surprisingly hard to focus on your heart for three full breaths without your mind drifting. You can do this exercise anywhere, any time. Give it a try right now.

There are many ways to connect to your heart. Some take less time and some take more. When you are ready to connect to your heart, remember that where your attention goes, your energy flows.

6

PERSONAL LISTENING PRACTICE

It is possible to listen anywhere and any time. All you need to do is focus your energy on the present moment, tune out your surroundings for a moment, and tune into your emotions, thoughts, and bodily sensations.

Personal Listening Practices come in all shapes and sizes. Listening is about training yourself to become hyper-aware of yourself on multiple dynamic levels. Listening requires you to monitor the invisible field of energy created by the mind, body, and emotions. This is important because your inner life creates your outer reality. If you want to change your reality you must change how you think, feel, and act.

What you gain by listening to yourself over time is integrating the typical fragmented parts of yourself into a unified whole. This vibrant, healthy inner ecosystem enhances your ability to make better decisions that align with your values and build confidence to trust yourself more.

I often use the singular "yourself" when referring to you, but it would be more accurate to use the plural yourselves because your mind is made up of many different parts. This idea is called multiplicity of the mind. It is essential to understand this concept as you learn to listen to yourself. Listen to my interview on The Soul Games/Unravel podcast[13] for a more detailed explanation of multiplicity.

When I refer to you having parts, I want you to think of the many roles you play in your life. A few examples might be mother or father, professional artist or athlete, CEO or employee, brother or sister, son or daughter, friend or lover.

It is common for different parts of you to disagree, creating internal conflict. This conflict arises when parts want opposite things regarding the same topic. For example, if you are dating someone, one part might want to break up while another argues for staying together.

An important part of listening to yourself is discerning which part of you is trying to get your attention and what that part needs. Whenever you have a strong emotion, that is one of your parts trying to get your attention.

When parts disagree, it is no different than when people disagree. They must communicate to work out their differences or a rift develops. If this rift is not repaired, it will create inner turmoil.

Remember, as you begin your *Personal Listening Practice*, there will be many voices in your head vying for attention. As Richard Schwartz, the creator of Internal Family Systems, says, there are no bad parts. Each part of you is important with something valuable to contribute to your mental health and overall well-being. Treat them as you would treat a member of your family that needs help.

Fostering a healthy relationship with your mind is not the only reason to start a listening practice. Learning the discipline of listening to yourself provides you with a source of grounded guidance rooted in your intuitive wisdom. You should *never* give that power of freewill and choice away to someone else. Doing so will inevitably lead you down a path of chaos and disorder.

As a teenager, my father bought me a twelve-cassette self-improvement program called *Lead The Field* by Earl Nightingale. On one of the cassettes, Nightingale tells the story of a farmer. This farmer kept hearing stories about other farmers in the area getting wealthy by prospecting for diamonds. Operating with irrational exuberance, the farmer sold his land and everything he owned and embarked on an adventure to find diamonds and get rich.

The farmer spent the rest of his life searching for those elusive gems. At the end of his life, he became so despondent over his bad luck and misfortune that he threw himself into the river and died.

Several weeks after buying the farm from the farmer who went off prospecting, the new owner wandered around his property when a bright flash of blue light from a nearby creek caught his eye. He picked up the rock and liked it so much he put it on his mantle.

Sometime later, a friend came to visit. While they talked, the friend noticed the rock. He picked it up and nearly fainted. He knew the farmer had found an enormous diamond of great worth. The farmer said this was the biggest one, but there were smaller ones just like it scattered throughout the creek on his property. He thought they were inexpensive crystals.

This story continues to have a lasting impact on me. The meaning is obvious and profound. You are the farm with hidden gems lying all around in plain sight. Those diamonds are your intuitive wisdom. You can discover hidden treasures deep within yourself with focused effort and attention.

You have lived a lot of life. You have learned much along the way. You have more than a few harrowing experiences under your belt. Each life experience can be used to build your intuitive wisdom, helping you make wiser decisions, if you allow yourself to heal and use those experiences for your benefit. You must do the work to craft your intuitive wisdom into a work of art, much like a master luthier transforms raw wood into a musical instrument.

Each of us carries baggage from our past that we regret. We've stayed in a relationship too long, causing ourselves way more pain and suffering than necessary. We lost a friend over a minor disagreement. We made a poor financial decision that haunts us to this day. How do you begin to recover and trust yourself when your best thinking got you into some of the worst predicaments of your life?

Here are several points to consider.

First, many of your worst decisions were made when you were younger and less mature. If you didn't get anything else from those difficult experiences, you at least learned what not to do in the future. That's something.

Second, you often beat yourself up for bad decisions, but the truth is that while you may have known better now, you may not have known better then. You did your best with the information and experience you had at the time. Even if you knew better, you had your reasons for doing what you did. You wanted something more than you wanted to make the wise decision. It was likely related to your ego seeking instant gratification rather than delaying gratification. Some of life's most important lessons come from our most painful mistakes.

Third, you most likely had no *Personal Listening Practice* during those times of poor decision-making. How much time each day did you dedicate to listening for solutions to the problems you were facing?

Fourth, one of the biggest causes of adverse outcomes is your blindness to what you don't want to see. When you don't want to see a solution because it conflicts with what you want, you cut yourself off from your intuition. While this is temporarily appealing, it always causes more problems than it solves.

Fifth, look at you now! Here you are, doing your work, trying to correct your past errors in judgment by reading a book about how to listen to yourself. That shows you are learning, growing, maturing, and evolving. By the time you finish this book you will have a plan for how to handle challenges and learn to trust yourself more.

Even after all of your past missteps and poor decisions, returning to listening to yourself to help you make informed decisions will heal the wounds from your past. You are never too far gone to start living by the virtues of love, wisdom, and integrity. Each day is a new opportunity to begin that journey anew.

You heal your past by acknowledging your mistakes and committing to doing the work today to become a better person.

7

ROADBLOCKS TO LISTENING

This chapter is long because the ways you can sabotage yourself and your *Personal Listening Practice* are endless. Here are some of the more common ways and what to do about them.

GETTING PAST THE NOISE

One of the most common obstacles to listening is sticking with it long enough to get past the noise of life. Life is noisy and no matter how long you practice listening, this nonstop cacophony will never completely fade. The noise is simply another test of your dedication to learning how to listen to yourself.

So much about living a beautiful, peaceful, vibrant life is about being present to what is happening right in front of you *despite* the noise and distractions. Sticking with your practice long enough to get past the noise and settle down is a necessary right of passage to succeeding.

PERFECTIONISM

The pursuit of perfection is a vicious trap. It is a quest for an imaginary prize that literally never materializes. Just before reaching your objective and celebrating your accomplishment, the goalposts move and you're back to square one. You never achieve perfection because it is a mirage. It doesn't exist.

The hidden agenda behind perfectionism is a never-ending, frustrating, demoralizing loop. Perfectionism is unattainable; therefore, a constant feeling of failure perpetuates trying harder. The pursuit of perfection is the inner critic's playground. The sneaky secret of perfectionism is that we are fed these lies from a very early age through subtle and not so subtle indoctrination in a culture of bigger, better, faster.

The good news is that it only takes a slight inward adjustment to transform this self-destructive mindset into a positive, affirming practice. Once you recognize you are on the neverending hamster wheel of perfection, all you need to do is get off and get on the path to pursue excellence.

The pursuit of excellence is a worthy endeavor because it carries the thrill of improvement and achievement but without all the toxic negativity of perfectionism. Those who are pursuing perfection and make a mistake will inevitably speak cruel harsh words over themselves. "I'm so stupid. How could I miss that shot? I'll never be good at this. Everyone else is so much better. I should just give up." Someone who learns to pursue excellence has a different mindset. They see failures and setbacks as part of the road to success. They love themselves and treat themselves accordingly. Those who strive for perfection are constantly disappointed in themselves and carry the baggage of self-hatred everywhere they go.

The pursuit of excellence is a place where you give your maximum effort and then let go of the rest. It is where you celebrate your achievements and thoughtfully set realistic new goals. It requires an inward perspective shift more than any outward adjustment. It would be difficult to pick out someone pursuing excellence versus someone pursuing perfection based on external actions alone. Their behaviors look similar. Spend any time around these two individuals and it would soon become apparent which one is which. Don't let the disease of perfectionism creep into your listening practice. The only way to get it wrong is by not trying. Otherwise, you are golden.

The best way to determine which camp you fall into is by listening to your inner dialogue about anything. The inner critic has no problem criticizing everything from your body, your parenting, to how you drive to work, your bank account, your tennis game, or your love life. It will latch onto anything it can. The pursuit of perfection sees only lack. It focuses its energy on what you have failed to accomplish. The pursuit of excellence measures your progress by your effort and attitude.

If you are a perfectionist, my only advice is to stop. It really is that simple. You need no special skills or secret wisdom. Replace your self-critical inner dialogue with positive, affirming statements about how you are making progress and learning new skills which takes time. Celebrate your successes and the effort you put in every day. Give yourself a "Nice Job!" when you deserve it and go splurge on yourself. Be grateful for a healthy body and mind to be able to create something original.

If you think this sounds like an overly simplistic solution to a complicated problem, that's just your inner critic trying to distract you. The hardest part of making this transition will be silencing your inner critic. Changing deeply ingrained habits takes work, but changing any self-destructive behaviors takes work. Why not focus on something that will make your life easier instead of harder, happier more than disappointed?

DISTRACTIONS

Here in America, we excel at finding ways to distract us from our inner life. There is always a new movie or TV show premiering. There is a constant cycle of one sporting event ending with another ramping up. We have New Year's in January, the Superbowl in February, baseball and tennis in the spring, summer concerts, and vacations with the kids before school starts in August. There are early school drop-offs in the mornings, team practices in the afternoon, and the beginning of the NBA, NHL, and NFL season in the Fall. Before you know it,

October, November, and December are here and gone, and we are back where we started. Where does the time go? In addition to this long list are family gatherings, birthdays, graduations, engagement parties, weddings, church attendance, and funerals.

This is the macro view of our busy lives, but what about the daily distractions you face? You wake up and go to the gym or take a run while listening to a podcast or book before hitting the shower and making it to work just in time for the team meeting. Work takes up much of your day, only to rush home to cook dinner for the family before soccer practice and Boy/Girl Scouts. The days fly by with us on autopilot. Wash. Rinse. Repeat. Where exactly are you supposed to fit in a practice that requires you to sit still and be quiet?

It is easy to understand how this Groundhog Day lifestyle can become a depressing cycle. It's so full, yet leaves you empty if you are not paying attention. To keep the freight train that is your life running on time, you take a feel-less-bad pill that doesn't fix anything. It only numbs you so you can continue to be a functioning adult. You wonder why your sexless marriage is faltering and the only joy you feel is unconsciously living vicariously through your children. Then, one day, you find yourself in the emergency room thinking you're having a heart attack. Your heart is fine. Your mind is panicking.

Familiar distractions are hard to overcome because they feel immovable. What are you supposed to do, pull the kids out of sports? Quit your job? Get a divorce? Move back in with your parents at thirty-eight?

If you want to slow everything down and start listening to yourself, you must make sacrifices, which will be uncomfortable. Something will have to give because every minute of your day is spoken for by someone or something.

The secret to managing the chaos is to start small and go slow. You are not competing in a race. You can even make the weeks of preparation to create your *Personal Listening Practice* as part of your listening process.

During the planning phase, you can find a favorite spot or three in and around your house where you will go to listen. Different spaces for different seasons of the year are a simple way to keep your listening experience fresh. Buy something living, like a bonsai tree or an orchid, to bring life and beauty to the space. If it is not well-lit, buy a lamp with light bulbs that give off a warm glow. Candles are a great source of warm light. Don't underestimate the power of light in your space[14].

Start your day by listening in your *Sacred Space*. Do this at the same time each day. You can prioritize your practice by adding it to your reminders or work calendar. This way, you get a notification encouraging you to practice.

Buy a journal and a box of pens. If you can afford them, noise-canceling headphones are beneficial if you live in a busy household or have roommates. Now, all that is left to do is to get started. This sacred time might become your favorite part of the day.

PERSISTENT NEGATIVITY

Did you know you have the power to choose to bring hope and optimism into *any* moment? Do you believe that is possible? Yes, some moments might not be appropriate for a full-on display of exuberant joy, but even in those dark moments, you can bring in love and hope through silent support and a loving presence.

We are a cynical and pessimistic species. It kept our ancestors alive by remaining hypervigilant, always being suspicious of every strange sound and unknown object was how we survived. Today, you still carry this survival instinct but, thankfully, without as many ever-present threats. If you aren't careful, this once useful survival mechanism can unconsciously brand anyone who isn't in your tribe as an enemy.

Persistent negativity can erode your optimism and replace it with nothing of value. Negativity locks you into fear and keeps you isolated, adrift in the sea of hopelessness, never allowing you to come near the safety of the shore of community. This persistent negativity is not only towards those who look or believe differently than you. Eventually, you will turn this judgment on yourself, making you the focus of your self-loathing criticism.

The ultimate death blow of negativity is when you turn on yourself and become your own worst enemy. You fail to love others because you fail to love yourself. You fail to take care of others because you fail to take care of yourself. You must have the courage to look in the mirror and take responsibility for your thoughts and actions. You choose what you let in and you should be very cautious about what you allow past the mental gates guarding your heart and mind because what you allow in, you will become.

FEARS

The hits keep coming with each distraction and fear might be the biggest one of them all. You've heard it before, but it bears repeating: Fears are the only thing standing between the life you have and the life you want.

As you face your fears, they disappear. There is absolutely no need to take the healing journey alone. There is strength in numbers. The love you find in others can sustain you when you struggle. Love is and will always be stronger than any fear you have.

UNWORTHINESS

Unworthiness is the big sleeping giant in this little list of road-blocks. Unworthiness is the smoke that sneaks under the door of your heart and mind. Unworthiness is the belief that you don't deserve good things. This lie may have been transferred to you by a cruel, mean-spirited parent. It might have formed after the breakup of a long-term romantic relationship. Wherever this belief originated, it is seldom discussed and hard to untangle.

Logically, you know you are worthy of good things, but emotionally you feel the opposite. If you were to put this in the language of multiplicity, you would say one part of you feels unworthy of good things, but another part knows that is not true. This internal conflict creates internal chaos.

You manifest self-hatred by neglecting or abusing yourself. You have a toxic inner monologue of nonstop criticism, reinforcing your sense of unworthiness. In your isolation, you deceive yourself into believing everyone speaks to themselves in the same harsh, cruel manner.

While you freely heap this internal abuse on yourself, you would be devastated if you overheard your child being so self-critical. You would rush them to the nearest therapist's office and get them on a mountain of medications ASAP. You might even send them to a camp or inpatient care. You would move heaven and earth to let them know they are loved, loved, loved. You would try with great determination to communicate how much they deserve good things. But when it comes to you, that's a whole different story. It is easy for you to advocate for a friend or family member who needs encouragement, but it is hard to offer yourself the same love. Why? Because you don't feel worthy. Rarely do any of us listen to someone we don't like, especially if that someone is ourselves.

LAZINESS

Your parents and grandparents could be forgiven for not understanding the health benefits of mindfulness meditation, daily yoga routines, or weekly therapy sessions. While yoga has existed for thousands of years, Americans have only appreciated its benefits for a few decades. These and other similar practices, like breathwork, are a relatively new phenomenon in the Western world. Only after science gave the practices a thumbs up did the average American finally feel safe embracing these wild ideas.

Today, with the ubiquity of smartphones and the internet, ignorance is no longer a viable excuse. If you don't understand the mental and physical health benefits of mainstream exercises (i.e., running and lifting weights) and alternative treatments (i.e., ice baths and breathwork), then it is pure laziness.

There is a reason laziness (or slothfulness) is one of the seven deadly sins. It renders a person useless. Lazy people rarely fail at anything because they put forth so little effort. The failure to even attempt to listen to yourself blocks any growth from happening before it even gets started. It's the proverbial seeds on the stone path.

Laziness can hide in procrastination. Putting off till tomorrow what should be done today is a sure way to get your ticket punched for the pain train. Those who fail to prepare are often caught off guard by life. Someone failing to take action to foster their romantic relationship may be utterly surprised when a breakup or divorce happens. They may plead with their partner, "What did I do?!" Nothing and that's the problem.

HOPELESSNESS

Hopelessness is similar to persistent negativity, but it is different. Persistent negativity is seeing the negative in a situation or assuming the worst about someone right from the jump. Persistent negativity is hard to be around and even more annoying to live with, but it's not the end of the world.

Those who are hopeless are hovering over a dark abyss, barely hanging on to life. They are in crisis. I am no fan of psychotropic medications, however, in situations such as this, where a person's life is on the line, medications can positively impact their lives by easing their pain and helping them weather the storm.

If you feel you are in a crisis, call 988 right now. Make an appointment to see your primary care physician (PCP) right now. If you don't have a PCP, go to the nearest walk-in clinic right now. If you are contemplating suicide, don't do it. Ask for help from friends, family, or a therapist. Check yourself into an inpatient psychiatric facility. A few days' rest in a safe place will give you a new perspective. Once the storm passes, and the storm always passes, return to this book and begin your daily *Personal Listening Practice*.

ANXIETY

I have deep compassion for those who suffer from anxiety. Anxiety is a debilitating condition. Sitting still and listening to one's thoughts sounds absurd to someone whose mind never shuts off. They listen to endless mental chatter all day long.

Anxiety makes people want to run away from their mind, not toward it. Ironically, the cure for those who struggle with anxiety is in the problem itself.

Someone with a runaway mind finds it physically uncomfortable to be still and focus on their inner world. The bottom line is this: anyone struggling with anxiety can train themselves to be less anxious.

One problem those struggling with anxiety encounter is letting their mind run wild like an unruly child. Listening, meditating, journaling, and yoga are all effective ways to slow down the monkey mind and get it under control through breathing techniques, mental practices, body movements, and expressing emotion via therapeutic writing. I admit listening is more challenging for those who struggle with anxiety. Still, I suggest they have the most to gain from starting a regular *Personal Listening Practice.*

The true purpose of listening to yourself is to build a trusting relationship with yourself so you can learn to love yourself in a more profound, lasting way. This love will guide you to achieve what you most desire. This is the great reward waiting for you.

8

PREPARATION FOR LISTENING

The following suggestions will fortify your listening practice. It isn't necessary to master each idea before you begin. It is far more important to get started and add these as your practice develops.

ELIMINATE ALL NEGATIVE THOUGHTS

Eliminating all negative thoughts is a great way to live your life. This one practice alone can radically change your life for the better. This process will be discussed in greater detail in the chapters on *The Transformational Path*. The most effective way to eliminate negative thoughts is by replacing every negative thought you have with something truthful, honest, and encouraging. You may not have control over what comes into your mind, but you certainly have control over what you allow to linger there.

Your mind is complex and powerful, storing every memory in its vast database. To illustrate the magnitude of your mind's potential, let's do a thought experiment. Think about your bedroom as a child. What kind of sheets were on your bed? What color were the walls painted? Were there any pictures and posters on the walls? What else was in your room besides your bed? Did you have a chair, table, or a box full of toys? What was underneath your bed? Was it a bunk bed? Did you share your room with a sibling?

How long has it been since you thought about your childhood room in such detail? A day? A year? A decade or more? Yet you could recall so many details in a few short seconds. Where were those memories thirty seconds ago? They were buried deep in your unconscious, just waiting to be retrieved.

Now, think about the many good, bad, and neutral memories stored in your brain. Each needing only a slight nudge via an image, sound, or smell to bring it rushing to the surface. This is the power of your unconscious mind and why you must consciously choose what you allow to linger in your mind.

It is important to differentiate negative thoughts from traumatic memories that need healing. One example of harmful thoughts is called catastrophizing. Catastrophizing is when you make up false narratives based on your fears and insecurities then let those thoughts run wild. These falsehoods have no basis in reality and are extremely destructive.

An example is rushing to the idea that your partner must be cheating on you when they don't answer your phone calls or texts. If there is a history of infidelity, this fear may be warranted. However, if no such history exists, you risk irreparably damaging your relationship by giving in to your fears.

It is better to learn how to soothe yourself rather than hoisting this burden of your fears onto your partner. If you run to them whenever you feel anxious, upset, or worried, expecting them to always take care of you, you miss opportunities to advance your own personal growth. You will eventually exhaust your partner and their goodwill, jeopardizing the relationship. You must correct this disruptive behavior if you want to have a healthy, strong relationship.

A better way to handle this situation would be to retreat to your *Sacred Space* and honestly admit your fears are real to you but unfounded in reality. Recognize this as a negative coping mechanism you use to get your needs met, but now you are ready to let go of this harmful behavior.

The source of the problem is that you feel lonely and scared. This could be based on being abandoned in past romantic relationships. It could also stem from abandonment issues from childhood due to a neglectful parent. All you are trying to do is get your needs met by panicking and creating a problem where a problem didn't exist. You will seriously damage your relationship if you rope your partner into this tailspin by incessantly calling and texting, demanding they video call you to prove where they are or begging them to come home.

Once you are in your *Sacred Space,* use distancing language such as "you" and "your." For example, you might say, "Reb, your partner loves you. Reb, you can trust them. Reb, you will choose to believe the best about your partner. Reb, by trusting your partner, you are loving them. Reb, the made-up story about them cheating is a lie." As you speak truth over yourself, control your breathing by slowly inhaling and exhaling. This will calm your nervous system.

You may be tempted to try and eliminate traumatic memories the same way but that would be a mistake. If you are repeatedly over-whelmed by intrusive memories of an abusive relationship, for example, trying to eliminate those thoughts is unhealthy. Those thoughts are coming to the surface for a reason. It is in your best interest to work with them. Pushing memories away is called suppression. This coping strategy will eventually make you mentally and physically sick. Negative thoughts are not the same as traumatic memories.

Eliminating negative thoughts is a manual process, like eliminating termites in your crawlspace. Through regular maintenance and check-ups, you would inspect your home for infestations. Once identified, you would use the proper tools and chemicals to kill and remove the pests. You would then make repairs to fix any damage.

It may be necessary on occasion to use brute force to eliminate negative thoughts. There is often a chicken or egg problem when it comes to negativity. If you experienced a life-altering trauma, it could have lingering effects on your mental well-being long after the actual incident. An example of this kind of prolonged trauma is the untimely death of a spouse. You may have been a fun, easy-going person before their death, but the loss sucked you into a black hole you cannot escape. This kind of negativity has the problem of altering the brain so that negativity, fear, pessimism, and hopelessness begin to take root and depression becomes your new norm.

It is nearly impossible for someone in such dire straits to pull themselves up by their own bootstraps. They need support from friends and family but may also require the brute force of medications, psychotherapy, support groups for grief, inpatient hospital stays, a month-long retreat, EMDR, hypnotherapy, to name a few treatments. All these strategies take time, money, discipline, and effort, but they may be necessary to get out of the chicken-and-egg loop.

Let's return to eliminating the everyday, run-of-the-mill negative thoughts like being judgmental and critical of others. It is easier than you think to redirect your negative energy into a more positive expression. All it takes is a little effort to identify the subject of your negativity and then transform whatever you are being negative about into something positive.

Let's say you are shopping at the grocery store, and you come buggy-to-buggy with someone wearing a t-shirt espousing very different political views than yourself. As soon as you see the t-shirt, your blood pressure spikes, and the wheel of negative thoughts starts churning. Your internal dialogue switches from which pasta sauce to buy for dinner to something dark and vengeful. You think about all the harmful decisions people who subscribe to those political beliefs have caused you and others. You ruminate on how "those people" must be stopped or they will "rip our nation apart." All of this happens in a matter of seconds, not minutes. You have whipped yourself into a frenzy right there on aisle six! What a tangled web we weave when we practice negativity.

Brute force tactics are helpful in these situations. You must immediately stop your negative, hate-filled, judgmental thoughts as soon as you notice them. Remember, you aren't responsible for the ideas that come into your mind, only those you allow to linger. The question remains: How do you stop a runaway train of thought? You can't. The answer is to get on another train. There is no redemption on the pain train of self-destructive thoughts.

Getting on a different train of thought can take a heroic effort. In the example of our grocery store standoff, you may feel a sense of superiority over this individual. You may feel you are on the side of good fighting evil. Yet the reality you have constructed is fiction, not fact. The truth is that this other person is just like you and has reasons for believing what they do. No amount of shopping cart thuggery is going to change this person.

The only way to overcome habitual patterns of negativity is to level up your game. Stopping any negative thoughts prevents you from going down a rabbit hole of hate or doing something you regret. However, controlling your negative thoughts is not enough. Your heroic willpower cannot go on indefinitely.

You have the power to transform any negative situation to your benefit. In this example, you can resist the impulse to lash out even if that lashing out is done only in your mind. Your efforts to transform the situation to your benefit may be to send your aisle six enemy a blessing instead of a curse. Yes, that's right. A blessing!

By blessing, I mean wishing them well in life and love. An example of a blessing might be, "May you have a peaceful day. May you know that you are loved." This simple practice requires expert-level self-control and self-awareness. Doing this isn't easy until it is easy. Then, when it's easy, it's easy. See how easy that is?

EXERCISE. EAT WELL. GET REST. FLOSS.

Regular exercise, a healthy diet, and consistent quality sleep are all good advice, whether from your mother, a doctor, or a book. In his book *Outlive*, physician and podcaster Peter Attia claims these three habits are hands down the best medicine you can give your body. Period. No medication or medical intervention consistently outperforms these basic life practices. As for flossing, research shows that people who don't floss are twice as likely to have heart disease. I don't know that flossing is a miracle cure but people who floss are probably more likely to engage in other healthy habits so start flossing to improve your *Personal Listening Practice*[15].

The reason these habits are good for listening is the same reason they are good for living. They form the foundation of a healthy body and healthy mind. I am reminded of the quote from Greek physician Herophilus, "When health is absent, wisdom cannot reveal itself, art cannot manifest, strength cannot fight, wealth becomes useless, and intelligence cannot be applied."

Start exercising today. Don't wait for the perfect plan, time, or weather. You can order resistance bands or weights on Amazon or go to the gym and bulk up with heavier weights. You can walk your dog an extra mile or train for a half marathon. You can hike with a friend in a park or climb all the 14,000-foot mountains in Colorado. If you exercise with other people, you are double dipping into multiple healthy behaviors by exercising and enriching your social connections. You can drink less alcohol, eat more fruit, and cook more meals at home. Whatever you do, get started now. Put down this book and take a walk.

LISTENING TO YOUR TIME AND MONEY

Like exercising, eating well, and getting good sleep, knowing how you spend your time and money is not a new idea. It may seem far afield from the practice of listening, but increasing your financial fitness can have a profound impact on your physical and emotional well-being. Many people are afraid of knowing where they spend their time and money. As a result, they waste both. When you figure out where your money goes, you'll know where your time goes. They go hand-in-hand.

You may solve many of your anxiety-inducing problems when you become aware of the flow of your time and money. If you feel frazzled because there is not enough time in a day or stretched too thin with too much month at the end of the money, then this type of "listening" is meant for you.

Knowing where your money goes may seem like Life 101, but that doesn't mean you know how to do it. Finances are intimidating. Money management skills, or a lack thereof, impacts every area of your life. Research shows those who track what they eat lose more weight than those who don't. The same principle is true for time and money. If you track your money, you are less likely to spend recklessly.

Suppose you realize you spend six hours a day on social media (and you don't run a social media-based business). In that case, you can redirect your energy to reading a book, connecting with friends and family, or writing a business plan for your dream business.

Your net worth impacts your self-worth. If you are underpaid at your job but resist discussing the topic with your supervisor because you loathe confrontation, you are leaving money on the table that is rightfully yours. Your employer is not responsible for ensuring you receive the highest possible salary.

The other side of the coin, pun intended, is the money going out, not just coming in. Listening to your finances means you check your bank account, credit cards, and investments regularly. You may only check your retirement account once every three months, but you might check your bank account several times a week. Knowing what comes into your bank account and what goes out may be stressful initially, but it will ultimately become empowering.

Being knowledgeable about your finances frees up mental space for more pressing matters. The insights gained by knowing where your time and money go will show you what you truly desire. It will offer insight into what to focus on during your *Personal Listening Practice.*

9

PRINCIPLES OF LISTENING

One of the benefits of a *Personal Listening Practice* is increased intuitive awareness. By consistently engaging with yourself on topics that matter to your life, you gain fresh insights and new perspectives that are more nuanced than the solutions that are obvious to everyone. As a result of going deeper within, your emotional intelligence increases and your parasympathetic nervous system becomes an ally.

Several general principles will help synchronize your body and mind for an optimal listening experience. These guidelines work for any type of listening, but the kind I recommend most is a time set apart each morning to reflect on your life through journaling and listening in silence. These are suggestions based on personal and professional experience over many years. I encourage you to create strategies that work best for you.

IT TAKES TIMES

As mentioned previously, the number one obstacle to a successful listening practice is giving up. On the positive side, the majority of clients do attempt starting a *Sacred Space* practice. On the downside, the majority also give up within a week or two. The reasons why people quit vary, but many fail to see immediate results and convince themselves they are doing it wrong. They stop and never return to the practice.

Any worthwhile endeavor requires study and commitment to see any real benefit. Angela Duckworth calls this stick-to-itiveness grit. Her research revealed that grit, defined as "passion and perseverance for long-term goals," is the core of what it means to endure hardships and achieve success.

SAME PLACE. SAME TIME.

We are creatures of habit and we create habits because they calm us down and give us a more efficient way of accomplishing tasks. The same is true for your *Personal Listening Practice* and that is why I recommend removing as many obstacles as possible when getting started.

One way of doing this is by listening in the same place at the same time. It is helpful for your *Sacred Space* to be organized and ready to go when you arrive. Make sure your AirPods and phone are charged. Clean up the clutter the night before.

When you create *Sacred Spaces* around your home, your body and mind will begin to associate those places and that time with listening. After several months of consistent practice, your mind will preemptively start listening before you arrive in your big, comfy chair. It is a subtle but powerful priming effect like a ritual.

Sitting in the same place at the same time every day isn't necessary, but consistency in these areas will enhance your experience. You may have several spaces or places you go for your listening sessions. Each will be valuable for different reasons and in different seasons.

THE DAWNING OF THE DAY

This principle is true for most people but not practical for some. For example, if you are a nurse who works the night shift from 7 PM to 7 AM, an early morning practice isn't practical due to the inverted work schedule.

When it comes to a *Personal Listening Practice*, morning is not a time of day as much as when you wake up. So, for our nurse friends and others like them, if you wake up at 3:00 PM, that time is your morning.

The reasons why mornings are the optimal time for listening are apparent. Hopefully, you are well rested. It is the start of a brand new day. You get to make this day whatever you want. Reflecting, listening, and planning first thing in the morning is an excellent opportunity to craft your day to your liking.

It may be necessary to adjust your wake-up time thirty minutes earlier to have enough quiet time before your busy household starts to wake up. Nothing sabotages the stillness of a listening session more than someone yelling, "Where's my shoes?" from across the house as if you are the keeper of all things footwear.

WHAT YOU THINK ABOUT YOU BRING ABOUT

This is another idea with profound implications. It's a law of nature, like gravity. Whatever you allow to stay in your mind will ultimately be what you become.

One of the basic principles of listening is being intentional with your thoughts. One way of doing this may be to bring inspiring poetry, sacred texts, or uplifting music into your listening space. Reading motivating and encouraging ideas can give you a more receptive frame of mind for listening. Adding supplementary resources is like adding salt to your meal. You don't want too much or you will ruin it. If you spend most of your time reading, you won't have time to reflect and listen, which is the most important element of your listening practice.

DO IT EVEN WHEN YOU DON'T FEEL LIKE IT

This is a tricky one. As anyone who has ever built anything with wood or worked on an engine knows, if you force something out of frustration, it almost always ends in that thing breaking.

Perseverance is working through your resistance to achieve a worthy goal. We all know the stories of Olympic athletes who spent their youth waking up at three in the morning to start their training. They missed late-night parties with friends to have a chance of playing at the collegiate level and hopefully earning a spot on the Olympic team. It was difficult for them to wake up when it was below freezing and still dark outside. They wanted to win more than they wanted comfort. I want you to want to listen to yourself more than you want to stay in bed an extra thirty minutes.

YOU CAN'T LISTEN TOO MUCH

Blaise Pascal was a child prodigy. He grew up to be a mathematician, physicist, philosopher, and inventor in the 1600's. He famously wrote, "All of humanity's problems stem from man's inability to sit quietly in a room alone." This is still true for us today.

Listening is like drinking water. It is hard to drink too much water. Just as most of us could benefit from drinking more water, most people could benefit from listening to themselves more.

The real problem many encounter when starting a listening practice is not taking action on what is heard during the session. If listening distracts you from taking action, then you are listening too much and not acting enough. Ideas die on the vine when they remain in your mind. Listening without action is like pouring yourself a glass of the finest wine but never drinking it. What a waste.

10

HOW TO LISTEN

There are no right or wrong ways to listen. There are only good ways and better ways. You can listen anywhere you want, any time you want, doing anything you want. There are no rules on how long a session needs to be. You can listen while walking, running, driving, on a date, in a meeting, on vacation, playing a sport, or while falling asleep.

Listening is, first and foremost, an attitude of open-hearted curiosity combined with a focused intention to connect with your intuitive wisdom. Whatever you want to accomplish, listening will enhance the experience. The real power of listening is its ability to transform a mundane experience into something sacred.

Remember, you are the most important person you know. You are also responsible for every decision you make. You must listen to your innate wisdom to make the best decisions possible so you can live with a clean conscience and without regret. To do that, you must spend time alone with yourself.

As we begin understanding what listening to yourself looks like in real, day-to-day life, let's start with the science behind that little voice in your head. As it turns out, people experience listening to their inner voice differently. University of Nevada Psychology professor Russell T. Hurlburt, Ph.D. has mapped five distinct ways to describe the inner experience of listening.

The first category is *Inner Speaking*. When someone talks to themselves in this manner it is similar to what they experience when they talk outloud. The second category is *Visual Imagery*. These people see in pictures what the *Inner Speaking* crowd describes in words. The third category is *Emotion*. Some people feel their inner experience more than others and this becomes their dominant internal sensation. *Sensory Awareness* is the fourth type of inner listening. This type of listening relates to how the five senses translate into inner awareness. The fifth and final category is *Unsymbolized Thinking*. Hurlburt admits this type is difficult to describe. Instead of linear ideas like the logical progression of a sentence, this type of inner experience is more chaotic and random. For example, if someone needed to go to the grocery store, post office and buy some flowers they wouldn't make a mental list to check off. They might see an image of an envelope with a stamp that has flowers on it. Hurlburt concludes that all five types are equally common. People may use more than one type of inner experience while others may have all five.

MY SACRED SPACE AS AN EXAMPLE

My *Personal Listening Practice/Sacred Space* begins well before I sit down with my pen and journal. Years ago, when I was first given the gift of the three virtues, I decided on a triangle to symbolize the three virtues. I knew triangles would be everywhere and could serve as constant reminders of my allegiance to living the virtues everywhere, all the time.

My very first act after waking up in the morning is removing my triangle pendant necklace from the bedpost and putting it around my neck. This symbolic gesture orients my day toward the three virtues of love, wisdom, and integrity.

I meander downstairs to boil some water for my French Press. While the coffee is steeping, I make my way to my *Sacred Space* where my pen, journal, and computer are waiting. I don't typically use my laptop. However, while writing this book, I kept it nearby just in case inspiration were to strike.

NOTES APP ON MY PHONE

Sometimes I begin my *Sacred Space* time by journaling. Other times I start with the Notes app on my phone. I have a note named *Sacred Space* and it is here that I have amassed a collection of ideas, prayers, mantras, pictures, sacred texts, and personal items meaningful to me. In many ways it has become a digital shrine to assist my daily spiritual practice. I am constantly rearranging the entries, rotating the ones that speak to me the most in the current season of life to the top of the note. Each time I make an edit, it moves the note to the top of the list ahead of all the other notes which is helpful. I also recommend keeping, rather than deleting, older unused entries. They will serve as a time capsule you can review at the end of each year.

At the top of the list on my *Sacred Space* note is the prompt reminding me to start with *The Three Slow Breaths*[16] exercise. This has become increasingly important as a centering technique not only during my *Sacred Space* time but throughout my day. It serves as a reminder to slow down, get grounded, and pay attention.

PRAYER

I read somewhere once that prayer is talking to God while meditation is listening to God. That felt intuitively right to me when I heard it. Prayer seems to be a lot of thanking and asking. This is not wrong, but it is different from listening. However, prayer is more powerful than most people give it credit.

One bizarre example of the power of prayer can be found in a research study by Leonard Leibovici in 2001[17]. He used a double-blind, parallel-group, randomized control structure to create two groups of patients with bloodstream infections. The patients in the control group did not receive prayers. The patients in the intervention group received intercessory prayers. Intercessory prayers are those prayers said on behalf of another person.

The results concluded that "mortality in hospital, length of stay in the hospital, and duration of fever" were significantly less in the group that received intercessory prayer.

If this study seems like a no-brainer, then you are among the eighty percent of people in America who consider themselves religious or spiritual. People who believe in God are typically the praying type and believe their God can control events in the material world.

Here is the kicker to this study that is not so obvious on the first pass. Digging into the study a little deeper reveals an interesting detail. Those patients being prayed for were not currently in the hospital. They were patients four to ten years before the research study was conducted. The people praying were praying for patients in the past, not patients in the present. Talk about mind-bending. Think about the implications.

When I first heard about this study, I was astounded. I believe in prayer, but this took it to a whole new level. Peppered throughout my *Sacred Space* notes are verses about prayer, "*Don't fret or worry. Instead of worrying, pray. Let petitions and praise shape your worries into prayers, letting God know your concerns. Before you know it, a sense of God's wholeness, everything coming together for good, will come and settle you down*"[18].

In my *Sacred Space* note, I have a link to a YouTube video of the Lord's Prayer spoken in Japanese[19] superimposed over images of cherry blossom trees blooming. I don't speak Japanese, but I enjoy hearing the words I know well in another language. Also included in my notes are pictures of my children. I spend a few minutes blessing them.

Finally, I would be remiss if I didn't include one of my favorite quotes by Mother Teresa in the section on prayer. It gives clear, direct advice on a life of faith, "*People are often unreasonable and self-centered. Forgive them anyway. If you are kind, people may accuse you of ulterior motives. Be kind anyway. If you are honest, people may cheat you. Be honest anyway. If you find happiness, people may be jealous. Be happy anyway. The* good you do today may be forgotten tomorrow. Do good anyway. Give the world the best you have and it may never be enough. Give your best anyway. For you see, in the end, it is between you and God. It was never between you and them anyway."

JOURNALING

After completing the preamble of coffee, notes, and prayers, I grab my pen and journal. Unless you have an expensive journal lying around your house, I would discourage you from buying one. Expensive journals exert unconscious pressure not to waste any space and write something profound. This subtle influence discourages freeform silliness like drawing sketches or writing in a big, sloppy script that takes up half the page. I want you to feel free to experiment with different forms of expression while writing and not restrict yourself. Yellow legal notepads are a great place to start. They are inexpensive and available everywhere.

Eventually, I found the lines too constricting and switched to unlined Moleskine journals. These are more expensive than legal pads but are well made with higher quality paper.

My journaling style has evolved many times since I started years ago. I use different methods for different moods. I adapt what I am doing when I have a specific goal. During one six-week period, I stopped journaling and wrote a screenplay instead. I want you to find freedom and playfulness that allows your journaling to be fun and not a burden. I also recognize that starting a journaling practice from scratch can be daunting.

Here is one of several formats I use to journal. I start with *The Three Slow Breaths* exercise then when I am ready I begin by writing the date in the top left corner. Across the page, in the top right corner, I designate the time of day, such as MORNING SESSION.

There are four possible listening session times: Morning Session, Noon Session, Afternoon Session, and Evening Session. I don't listen four times a day. Usually, I manage only one. If I need insight or feel emotionally unsettled, I will work in a second session. I might attempt three on rare occasions, but I have never journaled four times in one day. I differentiate the time of entry because if I go back and journal again later, it helps me visually separate and organize the entries.

All my journal entries begin with the same two short statements. The first is, "Good Morning Team!" My team consists of various psychological parts, specifically any needing attention that day. Parts that regularly make an appearance are Rebel, my young boy part and the C.E.O., which is responsible for running my various businesses.

I am spiritually oriented so my team also includes God, spiritual guides (aka angels), and departed loved ones who I believe support, encourage, and guide me. I want to acknowledge their presence and seek spiritual wisdom and reassurance.

Below this acknowledgment, I write my morning mantra:

May I be loving
May I seek wisdom
May I act with integrity
May I have a courageous heart

I didn't set out to create a mantra. It just happened. I have grown very fond of it and now recommend people create their own. I find this ritual comforting and empowering. Below my mantra, I draw three long dashes:

———— ———— ————

These three dashes have multiple meanings. Their obvious purpose is to separate one section from another. More importantly, though, this is one more way I reinforce my dedication to the three virtues of love, wisdom, and integrity.

Under the three dashes, I often journal about whatever is top of mind. This is what most people think of when they hear the term journaling. In this section, write about whatever you want. You can write about your feelings, your work, your date last night, your exercise routine, or what you ate for breakfast. Anything is fair game. When I feel complete, I move on to a more structured journaling style that involves active listening.

Through trial and error, I developed a method for listening I call Q.A.N. (pronounced *kwon*)[20]. Q.A.N. is an acronym for *Questions, Answers,* and *Notes.* The idea is that the best answers come from asking good questions. I have included a list of questions to help you jumpstart the Q.A.N. process at the end of this chapter.

The first step in the Q.A.N. method is to write the letter Q and then circle it. Next to this, write a question about something you want to know. For example, you might ask, "What do I need to accomplish today for it to be a success?" Below this question, I write the letter A and circle it. Then I pause, place my hand on my heart, and wait for an answer to come. Sometimes I close my eyes. Sometimes, I let my gaze rest in the soft morning sky. Sometimes, I doodle on a blank page.

Sometimes, information will come quickly. Other times, it takes a while for thoughts to form. Then there are those times I hear nothing at all. If I have waited a sufficient amount of time, but all I hear is silence, I move on by writing an ellipsis (...) next to the circled letter A, indicating I tried. I have other exercises I can do and moving on will help me maintain my momentum.

There is no set amount of time I wait. I have been doing this for so long now I can feel when I am in a flow state and when I am not. If you are starting out, give yourself more time before throwing in the towel. If you stick with your practice, you will begin to recognize your patterns.

Let me say a word about the Notes section of Q.A.N. The Question and Answer sections are self-explanatory. You think of a question, write it down, get an answer, and write that down. Repeat this process until you have received as much relevant information as you desire. The Notes section is for information that may or may not be related to the question you asked. The Notes area is a place for you to jot ideas down so you don't forget them but can stay focused on the task of listening.

Sometimes, you will receive important information unrelated to your original question. As you relax your mind, the distractions of life fall away and you more easily bridge the gap between your conscious and unconscious mind. When you enter this state, you are activating the *Default Mode Network (D.M.N.)*.

When your brain is allowed to wander unfocused, the *D.M.N.* kicks in, syncing the brain's prefrontal, parietal, and temporal lobes. Common examples of when this system gets activated are during meditation, daydreaming, twilight space before falling asleep, driving long distances, and those A-Ha moments in the shower. In these mentally relaxed moments, solutions to long-standing problems can emerge out of nowhere.

When it comes to waiting for answers, I have found that if I start writing a door inside my mind swings open allowing relevant information to come through. The more patient I am with myself and the process, the more relevant information tends to come.

If I stick with a listening session long enough, it has its own rhythm and comes to a natural conclusion. The energy that so freely flowed from my pen comes to a natural rest like the ending of a song. When I feel this energy shift, I know it's time to pack up and move on with my day.

The Q.A.N. method is a great way to start your daily practice. It has a beginning, middle, and end. Having a clear objective, like a problem to solve, is helpful. As you practice, you will become more familiar with your rhythm and how to best connect with your intuitive wisdom.

One aspect of listening that I wish was different is how subtle the messages are that come to me. I don't have enough data to say if this is true for most people, but I suspect it is. All I know is I would prefer a megaphone when receiving messages, but I get a whisper. Only on rare occasions do I get a megaphone.

I understand why the answers need to come in whispers. To hear a whisper, you must be quiet. You must be still to create a space away from the noise and busyness of your daily life. Those who create a

Personal Listening Practice will gain insight, wisdom, clarity, and inner peace.

WALKING MEDITATION

Most days, I walk. I need to walk. I crave walking. I have had as many, if not more, profound insights while walking as I have had while sitting quietly in my *Sacred Space* time journaling. When I walk, several things happen. I exercise. I pray/meditate. I listen to some form of ambient music without any vocals. Check the footnotes for a link to my Spotify playlist[21]. These allow me to easily slip into a *Default Mode Network* state.

The purpose of music is to heal. Music can instantly create a mood and transport you to another dimension in a hot second. Unless you are walking in a natural setting away from the cacophony of modern life, I recommend music to escape into yourself and expedite a contemplative mood.

Walking has a cadence to it, like dancing. Arms swinging in unison with the legs, which act like a metronome, keeping perfect time. This rhythm creates a mild hypnotic state, especially in mountainous or wooded areas surrounded by water elements.

Listening while walking is a different experience than sitting quietly and journaling. The cadence of walking lulls me into a rhythm where my mind can wander. In these free-floating spaces, my unconscious becomes conscious with little effort. It is hard to walk and write, so I am free from any expectations to capture my thoughts on paper. If I receive something profound, I will take a moment and jot it in my *Sacred Space* note.

Try walking as a form of listening. You might not do it every day, but it may be an excellent alternative to keep your routine from becoming monotonous. If you get nothing else out of the experience, it is healthy for your body to move.

THE POWER GRID

So much of our lives is monopolized by the power game. Who has power? Who wants power? Who doesn't have power? Power is malleable like water taking many shapes and many forms molding itself to any situation.

If you are unaware of your power, you will inevitably give it away. Power might come in the form of wealth, beauty, or status. It can also come by coercion, manipulation, and force. Power can also come in the form of patience, humility, and generosity.

The absolute best way to avoid giving your power away to others in an unhealthy way is to become aware of your power, who you give it away to, why you give it away, what you gain by giving it away, and not taking other people's power in an unhealthy manner.

The *Power Grid* exercise is a straightforward journaling exercise that could lead to some profound insights. I have created a worksheet for you to download and use in your *Sacred Space* time.[22]

The purpose of this exercise is to regularly check in with yourself to see where you may be giving your power away so you can reclaim it. This requires self-awareness and self-awareness begins by asking good questions.

The *Power Grid* exercises consists of four questions:

1. *Who or what am I giving my power away to in my life?*
2. *Am I giving my power away to this person or thing in a healthy or unhealthy manner?*
3. *Who or what am I taking power from in my life?*
4. *Am I taking power away from this person or thing in a healthy or unhealthy way?*

At first this may appear like a simple exercise you could complete in a few minutes but dig a little deeper and you realize there is a long line of people (i.e. wife, mom, friends, etc.) and things (social media, alcohol, work, etc.) that you give your time to. Deciphering whether or not this is done in a healthy or unhealthy way might take some time.

Any power you give away in an unhealthy way you need to reclaim. You want to be as powerful as you have the right to be. Anything less and you are not living up to your greatest potential. Any more and you are taking power that is not rightfully yours. This may sound melodramatic but any power you are taking that is not rightfully yours will not end well.

WHAT TO DO WHEN YOU HEAR NOTHING

Listening assumes that there is something to hear. However, if you listen long enough, you will notice your experiences will fall into one of three categories. There are times when you will receive lots of information, times when you receive less information and times when you receive no information.

I don't have an explanation as to why this happens. I have listened long enough to know that while hearing nothing is annoying, it's like the weather in Tennessee. If you stick around a few minutes, it will change. I have come to accept hearing nothing is as much a part of the listening process as the whisper and the megaphone.

When starting a *Personal Listening Practice*, it can be discouraging to be met with a great wall of silence. You may begin to blame yourself, wondering if you are doing it right. If this is you, consider the following.

H.A.L.T.

The acronym H.A.L.T. stands for hungry, angry, lonely, and tired. If you are crabby, angry, upset, or out of sync with yourself or others, you should check in and eat an apple. Is your judgment clouded because you are angry? Have you been pushing yourself, not eating well, and spending sleepless nights cramming for an exam or preparing for a big presentation at a conference? You may need some rest. Are you sad, lonely, and depressed? All of these factors may negatively impact your listening sessions. They are a good place to start if things are not going as well as you would like. You might be surprised at what a hot bowl of soup with fresh bread and butter can do for you on a cold winter's day.

TRY LATER

Sometimes it just isn't the right time. Trying to force a listening session because you are in a hurry and desperately need an answer is like force-feeding an infant stewed peas. You'll most likely end up with a sloppy mess. Slow down. Take a break. Come back later.

ULTERIOR MOTIVES

Are there hidden motives you are not being honest about? After years of experimenting with listening, I began forming ideas about how to make this into a book, an online course, a small group, or a class. My listening sessions became fishing expeditions, looking for ways to map and market this process so I could make money from it. This wasn't wrong, in and of itself, but I wasn't being honest about my motivation. I stopped listening purely to connect with myself. I needed each step to show results so I could package it and teach it to others. In other words, I lost my objectivity toward the process due to my financial motivations.

UNWANTED INFORMATION

What do you do if you are listening and you hear something you don't want to hear? Always remember the truth is simple, always good, and never changes. "Always good" doesn't mean what you hear will be fun or easy. Hearing something you don't want to hear but need to hear can be "good". If what you hear falls outside those parameters, you can't trust it. If you hear something negative while listening, make a note of it, but avoid getting stuck on it. Don't allow it to occupy your precious mental real estate. Take it to your therapist or best friend. Don't keep it to yourself and suffer alone. A fresh perspective might be all you need to see the truth. Sometimes it's just the inner critic talking and you need to move away from that voice and toward the inner voice of love.

If you are religious, take the information to your preacher, priest, rabbi, or imam for spiritual insight. If you are inclined to pray, ask for guidance and wisdom on what to do with the information.

Another good strategy is to pause and verify. When you are listening and hear something disturbing, upsetting, or doesn't feel right, take a beat and return to the Q.A.N. method by asking, "Did I hear the message correctly?"

TOUGH LOVE

This is a hard one, but maybe what you are hearing is the truth, you just don't want to hear it. The sign that this might be the case is if your body tells you one thing, but your mind tells you another. One way your body will show you whether or not you are mentally ignoring the truth is if your body deflates like a balloon when you think about the message you received. Your mind can work hard to convince itself the information is untrue. However, when you finally admit this terrible information *might* be true, your body will instinctively release its tension.

DO NO HARM

Here is a good rule of thumb to follow when receiving information: If what you hear causes you or someone else harm, you should not follow it. Pain is not the same thing as harm. Pain is sometimes necessary. Harm causes someone to suffer and is always unnecessary.

Q.A.N. QUESTIONS

Use this list to jumpstart your listening process. Remember, the best questions will ultimately come from within yourself. These questions are suggestions to help get you started. Only you know what you really want to know. If you find yourself uncertain about how to begin, start here. As is true with so many things, it's more important to get started.

1. What do I most desire?
2. What do I want to know?
3. What am I hiding or running from?
4. Where do I most need support?
5. What do I need to change about myself?
6. What needs to be healed in me?
7. Do I love myself?
8. What do I need to hear today?
9. Who in my life do I need to forgive?
10. Who in my life do I need to love more?
11. What do I need to start doing?
12. What do I need to stop doing?
13. What does it mean for me to live my life according to the virtues of love, wisdom, and integrity?
14. What needs to happen today for me to feel like it was a success?
15. Have I forgiven myself for past mistakes?
16. What obstacles are in the way of my success?
17. How can I love myself today?
18. How can I love others today?
19. Where do I spend my time and money?
20. Am I exercising enough, eating well, and getting enough rest?
21. Do I have inner peace?
22. What am I most afraid of hearing?
23. How am I allowing people to mistreat me?
24. How am I mistreating others?
25. What do I need to be working on right now?
26. Do I trust myself?

27. Do I feel safe with myself?
28. Is there anything else I need to hear before ending this listening session?
29. What will bring me peace?

11

MANTRAS

A mantra is a phrase with personal meaning you create to remind yourself of who you are, what you value, and who you aspire to be. It can be any length but the shorter it is the more likely you are to remember it, repeat it, and share it with others.

Your reality is manufactured from the substance of your thoughts because what you think about, you bring about. A mantra is a tool created by intentional mental effort to manifest an invisible truth into physical reality. If it is love you think about, it is love you will get. If it is revenge you think about, it is revenge you will get.

Mantras harness the power of your brain's 100 billion neurons and 100 trillion synaptic connections for your highest good. As legendary special forces warrior and spiritual guru Tu Lam says, "You need to understand body and mind is [sic] connected. You have to train the mind. The only way you reach a level of fulfillment and happiness is you train the mind."

It takes time to synthesize your thoughts into a bite-sized nugget. It doesn't matter if it takes six months. That is six months of you focusing on your core values, who you aspire to be, what matters most to you, and what areas of your life you need to work on. Once formed, mantras serve as an invisible amulet to protect you and remind you of the good work you are doing.

As your listening practice progresses you will develop tools to help you when you are tested or lose your way. It is helpful to think of your mantra as truth and light. Only the light can reveal the truth. In the light is love. In the darkness is fear. You will know you are in the darkness if you are confused, afraid, or making unhealthy decisions. Your mantra will be a light guiding you out of the darkness.

To create a mantra, pay attention to the patterns in your life. What themes keep repeating themselves? What causes you to stumble again and again? What activities do you engage in when no one is paying you? Mantras can be something you say for the rest of your life or created for temporary support to get you through a difficult season of life.

To be effective, your mantra should be repeated as often as possible. Your mantra is linguistic art and can find expression in many forms. It can be spoken out loud or in the quiet of your inner thoughts. It can be represented by a symbol or it can be written out in words. For me, a triangle came to symbolize love, wisdom, and integrity. I find as many ways as possible to incorporate my mantra into my life. One way I did this was to buy a necklace of a triangle pendant. First thing every morning I place it around my neck setting my intentions for the day.

When creating my mantra, I intentionally chose the phrase "May I" to convey a perpetual state of becoming rather than an objective to achieve. I can also easily adapt the wording of my mantra to bless others by changing "I" to "You".

PART TWO

12

SACRED MOUNTAINS

There is a photograph of me and my climbing partner on the summit just above St. Mary's Glacier in northwestern Colorado[23]. The picture was taken using a film camera before smartphones. There was no posing until the perfect moment was captured. You got what you got and wouldn't know what you got until much later.

My friend was moving from Nashville to Texas for college. After some discussion, we agreed that a detour through Colorado for mountaineering training was just the adventure we needed.

In the photograph, I am covered from head to toe in cold-weather mountaineering gear replete with ski goggles, wool mittens, and a water bottle dangling from the front of my backpack strap. On my feet are plastic boots with sharp metal crampons strapped to the bottom. These razor-sharp metal cleats kept me from slipping off the side of the mountain. You wouldn't know it by all the gear, but I am freezing.

My bright purple Gore-Tex jacket covers my heavily insulated down jacket, which I affectionately named "Big Puffy." At the moment the picture was taken, my toes were close to frostbite from standing in waist-high snow on the hours-long hike to the summit. It was winter and thick snow covered every peak.

In the photo, I am on my knees. My eyes are closed. My arms hang limp and my body slumps forward and slightly to the left as if the camera caught me about to face-plant unconscious into the rock-hard icy snow.

In addition to slowly freezing to death, I was also suffering from hypoxia, a lack of oxygen to my body and brain due to altitude sickness. We only gave ourselves one day to acclimatize from the 597 feet above sea level of Nashville to the 11,000-foot-high peak of St. Mary's Glacier. That was not enough time, but nothing could be done about the miscalculation.

It is a strange sensation to have the will to live slip away. I gave zero shits about anything. Maybe if I had kids or were married, I would have found some fight deep down, but at that moment, I only wanted to go to sleep forever. If I had allowed myself to rest, I would have died. After taking our picture, our guide noticed my deteriorating condition. He knew we needed to get down the mountain fast.

Somehow, I found the energy to stand up and put on my pack. I kept telling myself just one more step, then one more and one more. Our guide reassured me that I would start feeling better as we descended. He was right, and gradually, my life force returned.

Reflecting on our excursion and knowing what I know now, I would do it again. Why? I love mountains. I have been in awe of mountains since I was a small child. I can remember the moment when they transformed from geological formations created by the slamming together of continental plates into magical, mystical places.

I was five years old when my family drove from our small town in rural Arkansas down I-10 for twenty-five hours to Mexico City. I had never visited such a wild and chaotic place, and had it not been for my parents' quick hands and keen instincts, I would have surely been squashed by more than a few speeding motorists. Unfortunately, I had a penchant for walking into oncoming traffic without warning when no one was watching.

This was the 1970s and we were tourists doing touristy things. One of those touristy things was to ride a cable car up a mountain to get a bird's eye view of the city. I remember little of the ride, but I remember arriving at the top. This was the first mountain I had ever seen, much less been on top of. It did not disappoint. I was awe-struck by the ability to be so high and see so far. It was then one of the seminal moments of my life began to unfold.

It was a beautiful sunny day, which made the views from the observation deck that much more spectacular. As I looked down over the sprawling city, I noticed a big, white, puffy cloud slowly drifting toward us in the distance. I remember thinking how strange it was that the clouds were below us. "We are above the clouds!" my little five-year-old brain proclaimed.

The euphoria I felt in the sky above the clouds was intoxicating, but then something odd happened. The cloud continued on its trajectory until it collided with the side of the mountain and started crawling upwards like an avalanche in reverse. I remember feeling frightened because in my short life, clouds were those far-off objects, soft and fluffy like marshmallows. However, I realized I had never been inside a cloud, so I had no idea what they were actually made of. I'm sure it was just my primal instinct to be afraid of something big coming at me that I had never seen before, but I felt real fear, which may be one of the reasons I have such vivid memories of the experience. My apprehension didn't last long.

From a distance, the cloud appeared to be inching along at a snail's pace, but once it made contact with the mountain, it started racing in my direction. I realized that, for better or worse, this big, puffy, marshmallowy cloud would inevitably swallow me whole.

Before I knew what was happening, I was consumed by a hazy mist. The air changed from dry and hot to cool and damp. Then it hit my five-year-old brain, "I'm inside a cloud!" I felt an emotional mashup of a superhero mixed with a little bit of angel. I was in a cloud high in the sky. This has got to be what heaven is like, I thought.

In less than sixty seconds, the experience was over. The misty fog continued drifting away from us, but something changed. I was no longer the same little boy I had been before entering that cloud. I had been consumed by a cloud on a mountaintop, and now, something was different about me. The mountains were no longer just mountains. They were mystical places where magical things happened.

I am older now, and while I occasionally find myself on top of actual mountains, most of the mountains I climb now are different. The mountains I climb are still mystical and mythical, equally as dangerous, and formed by the tectonic pressures of life experiences. At fifty-one, I have summited a fair number of these personal peaks. I am much better at climbing these mountains now than I was when I was younger. I am also a guide, helping others ascend the jagged cliffs of pain and suffering to overcome challenges and find peace. I call these personal challenges *Sacred Mountains.*

Sacred Mountains can bring great joy or immense grief. Some of the more challenging mountains we all must climb are those experiences that rip our hearts apart, like losing a job, a marriage, or a child. We all have *Sacred Mountains* to climb in life.

Some *Sacred Mountains* are necessary, while others can be avoided if we do our work. At some point in most people's lives, they try to cheat the system and opt out of climbing their *Sacred Mountains.* They avoid the unavoidable sacrifice and struggle to conquer these formidable peaks until the pain is so great they can no longer avoid dealing with them.

Based on decades of experience, I have concluded people only change for two reasons. They either change by choice or by pain. Most of us wait and opt for the painful path only to face significant loss and soul-crushing pain. In those moments, we wish we would have chosen the other path, but by then it's too late.

Not all *Sacred Mountains* need to be full of pain and trauma. Some *Sacred Mountains* require effort, struggle, and sacrifice but are full of joy and hope, such as a healthy, strong marriage, raising children, staying healthy, starting your own company, and athletic or professional achievements. These, too, are *Sacred Mountains* where we give but also get back and, in the process, are rewarded. The more we choose to live with love, wisdom, and integrity, the more we experience this second kind of *Sacred Mountain*.

I have developed a map to help you navigate your *Sacred Mountains*. This map is a guide for how to transform your ordinary problems into something sacred. The path that ascends your *Sacred Mountains* is often challenging, with many obstacles along the way. There is another path, the easy one, and it leads down into the *Valley of Despair*. Many choose this path and wander around lost for a long time. It is a terrible place full of misery and hopelessness.

The *Valley of Despair* has consumed many lives. Its darkness holds power because sometimes it feels good to feel bad. However, you will more often be dragged into this wretched valley by a phone call at 3 a.m., an unprovoked act of evil, or an unfortunate prognosis from your doctor. Usually, it isn't your choice to go to the *Valley of Despair*. It is due to circumstances beyond your control. No matter how you end up in this terrible place, there is always a path out of the darkness waiting for you.

The consequence of staying too long in the *Valley of Despair* is chaos, confusion, and suffering. The longer you stick around, the sicker you become until you have had enough.

On the other hand, the benefit of choosing to make the trek up your *Sacred Mountain* is inner peace. I can guarantee with absolute certainty that the effort you put into climbing each of your *Sacred Mountains* will result in a reward that will ultimately bring you inner peace.

You can't climb a mountain without a backpack, or at least you shouldn't. You need food, clothing, shelter, tools, a medical kit, water, and a host of other supplies to help you stay alive in the hostile environment of the mountain wilderness. Danger lurks around every bend in the path. You could fall from great heights, bang your head against a rock, get mauled by a bear or bitten by a poisonous snake, or get lost and die of dehydration or hypothermia.

Backpacks are little temporary homes. A well-packed backpack can make the difference between having fun or having an incredibly miserable time. Nothing can take the place of a match, lighter, or flint striker when you are cold, wet, and hungry.

Every morning, when you put your feet on the floor and get out of bed, you are strapping on an emotional backpack full of memories. Your emotional backpack is stuffed with stories from your childhood, unhealed wounds, hopes for your future, your problems, your kid's problems, your work, your health, your successes, your failures, your secrets, your addictions, your spiritual life, your destiny, and your purpose to name just a few items you lug around every day. The problem with never unpacking your backpack is that it is tough to climb your *Sacred Mountains* while carrying around two hundred pounds of unresolved emotional weight. Do you know what's in your backpack?

Why would anyone go through the hassle of unpacking their emotional backpack? What you do with the stuff in your backpack will determine the quality of your life. Once you start climbing your *Sacred Mountains*, you begin to heal old wounds, seek forgiveness from those you have hurt, and let go of old resentments. You feel lighter.

When confronted with a decision, it may appear you have many options, but in reality, there are only a few. Each decision leads you up the steep cliffs of *Sacred Mountain* or down into the *Valley of Despair.*

Each day offers opportunities to choose one path or the other. Often, it isn't apparent which path leads where, but despite your lack of clarity, life demands you choose a path. How, then, do you choose? The way forward is to give your maximum effort, basing every decision on the eternal virtues of love, wisdom, and integrity, transforming your ordinary experiences into extraordinary opportunities.

13

THE
TRANSFORMATIONAL
PATH

Every man needs a plan if he wishes to be great because it is easy to get lost in the wilderness that is life. *The Transformational Path*[24] is a map that will help you navigate the rugged terrain of your *Sacred Mountains*. Nothing in *The Transformational Path* is complicated to understand or difficult to implement. It points you in a direction, gives you instructions, and lets you do the work.

The Transformational Path guides you step-by-step from problem to peace. It transforms a mundane obstacle into a sacred opportunity for growth by helping you embrace, instead of avoid, the seemingly relentless parade of challenges. Once you stop resisting and start embracing what comes your way, you gain power by taking control of your life.

The Transformational Path is laid out in a neat, tidy flowchart to help you see each step clearly and to make studying the process easier. However, as Mike Tyson is famous for saying, "Everyone has a plan 'till they get punched in the face." Life is going to punch you in the face. What you do once you get punched makes all the difference. That is when *The Transformational Path* can help.

I constructed *The Transformational Path* into a flowchart for the sake of simplicity. There is a pure quality to illustrating a complex idea into a simple image but I recognize this isn't how real life works. Problems introduce an element of chaos. If you do not have a plan for how to deal with that chaos you are inviting even more chaos to an already unstable situation.

If you are the type of person who likes to organize everything then feel free to walk step by step through *The Transformational Path* when you encounter a challenge. For the rest of us messier folks, it is best to use the steps as needed and don't worry about the order. I regularly find myself knee-deep in a life problem before remembering to use *The Transformational Path* and I am the one who created it!

The Transformational Path is not just a tool to use when you get in trouble. It has the power to help you prevent difficulties from ever happening if you learn to use it preemptively. By preemptive, I mean studying it during your *Sacred Space* time and practicing it in real life. How can it prevent problems? By infusing each step of the process with the virtues of love, wisdom, and integrity. This is what it means to live *The Sacred Life*.

Enough talk. Let's get started!

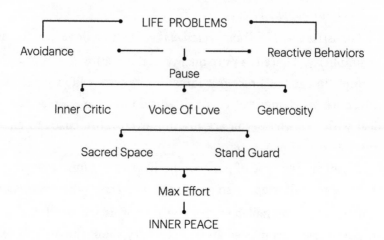

14

STEP ONE: LIFE PROBLEMS

At certain moments, we all experience life-changing events. Some of these will be wonderful, but some will be devastating. When overwhelmed with grief and suffering in pain, seeing how anything good could ever come from something so awful is nearly impossible.

Once we get some distance from the red-hot sting of loss, we pick up the pieces of our life and try to put them back together. We stumble into rich blessings like remembering the faces of those who were there in our darkest hour. They remind us we are not alone and we are loved. We catch a glimpse of the power and strength we possess to survive and continue living.

I experienced one of these devastating life problems years ago while going through a divorce. To say I was devastated would be an understatement. Even now, years later, with distance from that season of life, I can say with certainty I have never experienced anything more painful.

During this terrible time, I felt compassion for my wife. It wasn't like she gave up when things got hard. She stuck with our relationship for decades. There were many beautiful moments and even wonderful years along the way, but ultimately, she had to let go to move forward.

It would be impossible to untangle and explain the story of a twenty-year marriage. Attempting to do so would cause misunderstandings and more pain. Ultimately, we can only tell our side of the story.

During this time, I experienced relentless pain. So many questions harassed me hour after hour. How could I have let this happen? What was going to happen to the kids? How do I go on with life? On and on, the pain-filled days rolled into one agonizing blur.

Even amid this devastating pain, there were moments when I felt buoyed by love. I believed then and now I was being supported by friends, family, and guidance from the spiritual realm. When it comes to the veil between this world and the next, experience has shown me those closest to piercing that veil are those on the threshold of death and those suffering in great pain.

One way I found refuge during this terrible time was by walking in a park near our house every day. This beautiful three-mile loop surrounds a golf course with its spacious greenways and perfectly manicured greens. Along the western side of the trail is a tree-lined creek perfect for skipping stones.

Every day, as I walked the greenway, I prayed but mostly listened. I needed guidance, direction, solace, grace, and forgiveness. I needed healing because I felt I was sick and dying.

During this time, I listened to myself by holding a sacred space of silence. I was growing weary of asking myself unanswerable questions about why and how this happened. These futile questions drained my life force. I had to quit torturing myself and silence was my best option.

On one of these quiet listening walks, I had one of the most profound experiences of my life. The details of that day are etched in my memory. It was sunny and warm. I was making my way through the streets of our neighborhood to the greenway. This day felt like most days. It was very ordinary and very painful. Nothing gave any clue of what was about to happen. I walked. I listened. I hurt. I cried. I walked some more. I had not quite reached the greenway when an idea began to form like a gentle whisper. Then, I received a life-changing gift in the form of three simple words: Love. Wisdom. Integrity. The words appeared seemingly out of nowhere and as gentle as a whisper but they were unmistakably clear. I rolled the trio around in my mind, playing with their cadence and rhythm.

After a while, I started to repeat them out loud, "Love. Wisdom. Integrity. Love. Wisdom. Integrity. Love. Wisdom. Integrity." What did they mean? As I spoke each word, my body responded by calming down. I began to feel a peacefulness settle on me. The more I repeated the words, the more peace I felt. I was grateful for even the slightest relief from the relentless mental anguish.

Later on that same walk I was given a tiny little instruction manual that has to be the shortest ever written. The instructions were simple: From this day forward, live your life according to the virtues of love, wisdom, and integrity.

Problems suck. They disrupt the normal flow of life. They hurt. They don't stay contained in their little boxes even if you find the courage to face them. They end up causing other issues. Take losing a job as an example. The stress of prolonged unemployment can cause your immune system to take a hit, leaving your body more susceptible to infections and disease.

It is natural to try and shake off problems as quickly as possible. The only problem with this approach is that most speedy solutions only address the symptoms, not the underlying causes. This approach guarantees the same issues will resurface.

If you are going through a difficult season, know that redemption is possible, though it may be buried somewhere beneath the rubble of your tragedy. Healing is possible. Happiness is possible. Wholeness is possible. However, all of this depends on how you weather your storm.

When you commit to seeking truth and are willing to accept responsibility, your efforts will not be in vain. Your broken heart will heal. Your soul will learn the lessons it needs to mature. It is the seekers who are given the secrets. So, how do you get started fixing your problems? What do you do when you are facing overwhelming grief and loss? You have three choices.

15

STEP TWO: REACTIVE BEHAVIORS

Scan any best-seller list of self-help books and you are bound to find more than a few books on how to quell bad habits. One thing nearly all of our bad habits have in common is that they provide instant gratification and/or a temporary escape from pain. These self-sabotaging actions are called *Reactive Behaviors.*

Here are a few examples:

- Blaming others or refusing to take responsibility for your mistakes
- Controlling an argument by remaining silent or overreacting
- Verbal or physical violence or threats of violence against yourself or others
- Anger outbursts when anger is not the appropriate emotion
- Judging, criticizing, or demeaning others
- Criticizing displays of emotion in yourself and others
- Excessive use of alcohol or drugs to numb emotional pain
- Social isolation from others
- Engaging in suicidal and other self-harming behaviors

Reactive Behaviors always want instant gratification. If someone hurts you, you want them to feel your pain, so you hurt them back. The ego is at the center of this eye-for-an-eye storm. The ego gets reactive at the slightest insult. Think of the last time someone cut you off in traffic. What did you do? Honk? Flip them off? Swerve in front of them?

Not all *Reactive Behaviors* are, in and of themselves, destructive. Some are neutral, like alcohol. When alcohol is used with restraint, it can enhance an experience. Wine at communion during religious services is one example. However, when misused, alcohol becomes a problem, but alcohol isn't the real problem. It is the intention (or lack thereof) that makes the behavior healthy or unhealthy.

The most problematic consequence of *Reactive Behaviors* is that they inevitably funnel you right back into the same old problems you were trying to avoid by engaging in the *Reactive Behaviors*. This vicious loop only stops when you stop the *Reactive Behaviors*.

So many people choose *Reactive Behaviors* because they don't understand how to respond differently. Elevated behaviors often rely on delaying gratification, which requires suppressing strong emotions long enough to weather the emotional storm of a stressful situation. When this process doesn't happen, we do things we later regret.

To illustrate this point, imagine you are at a party with your spouse. Your partner has had too many drinks and is flirting with someone. You know they are flirting because there is light, playful touching and they are using their flirty laugh.

On the drive home, you confront them. In their inebriated state, they dismiss your concerns and laugh at you for being sensitive and jealous. Just for good measure, they throw in a haymaker by telling you to get over yourself. They aren't your property. They can do whatever they want.

A feeling of righteous anger overtakes you. Your thoughts turn vindictive. You start to say something but stop. Your partner sees you are trying to restrain yourself, but they goad you to say what is on your mind. You know speaking now will have disastrous consequences, but you are so angry and hurt you can't control yourself.

Your ego is wounded and wants to get even, so in a moment of temporary insanity, you blurt out, "I think we should consider divorce." Your partner looks at you, trying to determine if you're serious. You remain ice cold, looking straight ahead at the road.

As you predicted, your partner breaks down in tears. You enjoy the revenge momentarily, taking satisfaction in seeing their smug smile evaporate. The only problem is that now you can't unring that bell. You now live in a very different world than you did just a few minutes ago. You became reactive and indulged in that forbidden dark pool of vengeance.

The next day, there are apologies, more tears, and acknowledgment of your love for one another. But you are not out of the woods. You now have a choice on how to deal with the problem. You have a past littered with issues that you swept under the rug. You will likely repeat the same behavior, and eventually, the pattern will repeat.

LISTEN TO YOURSELF

This exercise will require you to do some soul searching. How do you get reactive in your life? What behaviors are immature, outrageous, and unacceptable? How do you fight with your partner? Do you fight fair or do you go straight for the jugular? How do you handle substances like alcohol or edibles? What about pornography or television? Do you tend to find as many ways as possible to escape your life or do you tackle problems head on? You are being given an opportunity right now as you read this book to change your life for the better. This is literally one of those crossroads moments yet it feels so ordinary. You're just reading a book. This is how *The Sacred Life* works. Life is filled with one ordinary moment after another. It is up to you to take these ordinary moments and make them extraordinary. You can do that by choosing to make some much needed changes and stop making excuses for bad behaviors. I told you this was going to require some soul searching. Get to it!

16

STEP THREE: WHAT ARE YOU AVOIDING

As a kid, I enjoyed going to the dentist because they doled out nitrous oxide (aka Laughing Gas) like candy. I remember the strange smell of the gas followed by the feeling of my body floating up off the chair. One day, while waiting for the Laughing Gas to kick in, I noticed a new sign taped to the wall. The quote read: *Ignore your teeth and they will go away.* It turns out the same thing happens with your problems. Don't give them any attention and they, too, will go away. However, like a cavity turning into a root canal, those problems inevitably return bigger, badder, and meaner.

Avoidance is just another *Reactive Behavior*, but its unique characteristics deserve its own category. Most *Reactive Behaviors* are action-oriented. They require you to physically take action. *Avoidance*, on the other hand, is passive.

Whatever you are avoiding today will turn into the chaos of tomorrow. No one wants chaos in their life. It only makes life messy and way more complicated than it needs to be. Why do so many of us avoid working on our problems?

The primary reason people avoid doing anything is because it's easier. That's it. *Avoidance* becomes a deeply ingrained habit. Related to this is our addiction to comfort. We worship comfort. *Avoidance* is the ultimate comfort. Why do the work today when you can put it off until never?

If you sincerely want to know what you have been avoiding, grab your pen and journal and take notes of the past year. Notice the people you have had fights with, the jobs you lost, the relationships that have ended, and the minor issues that are now major problems. The evidence is waiting for you whenever you are ready.

LISTEN TO YOURSELF

This is a particularly hard nut to crack. The act of avoiding makes it very difficult to notice what you are avoiding due to the fact that you are avoiding it. You have two options, get to the root of what you are avoiding or wait until the problem becomes so painfully overwhelming that you are forced to deal with it.

The best option is to do a simple, honest self-assessment by asking yourself the question, "What am I avoiding?" and then listen to what comes up and journal about it. If you are still stuck, ask a trusted friend or loved one. If that doesn't work, pay a professional.

17

STEP FOUR: PAUSE . . .
WHAT A PLEASURE

If getting reactive isn't the answer and avoiding your problems isn't the answer, what should you do when confronted with a *Life Problem?* Up to this point, we have discussed a lot of the ordinary and very little of the sacred. That changes now. *Pausing* is when something has happened and there is that brief moment, that window of opportunity, when you get to choose how you will respond. This will feel like every other annoying moment you have experienced, but it is anything but ordinary. It is an extraordinary crossroads moment pregnant with possibilities. You can either get reactive like you have done many times before or pause and choose a better path.

When you *Pause,* you transform the moment by showing restraint. You become stronger when you don't give in to negativity. *Pausing* will go against your primal instinct to attack what has attacked you. *Pausing* is your best option, but it is the hardest choice when emotionally triggered.

In his Kabbalah One class, David Ghiyam teaches, "What are you pausing? Pause your old patterns of taking energy to fill your lack." Whether you pause or not, you are creating your future in this sacred space. Will your future be filled with more problems, broken relation-ships, hurt, and anger, or will you choose to *Pause?*

What A Pleasure. What's the pleasure? Nothing! There is nothing pleasurable about going through a difficult or traumatic experience. But when you say *What A Pleasure*, you are saying, "I accept this. I will not run away from it. I will not get reactive. I will face it and transform this moment into something beneficial for my psychological and spiritual maturity."

There is no way to exaggerate the importance of *Pausing* in trying moments. *Pausing* is the door that leads you to the mansion of self-actualization. You cannot enter this grand palace through *Reactive Behaviors.* The door only opens when you *Pause.* To enter requires what will feel like heroic self-restraint, but that test only lasts for a few moments before your energy settles back down to normal.

What does it mean to *Pause?* To *Pause* when you want to react is the gritty, hard work of being a man or woman of integrity. When every cell in your body wants to lash out, be cruel, or put someone in their place, yet you choose to *Pause*, that is an example of profound wisdom in action. The Book of Proverbs says, "*Watch your words and hold your tongue; you'll save yourself a lot of grief.*[25]"

When you choose to *Pause*, you step into a state of suspended animation mentally and physically. So many of the unhealthy reactive behaviors you engage in are physical actions. By *Pausing* mentally and physically, you are giving yourself a moment to collect your thoughts and not do something you will later regret.

I love my children. Each is an incredible human being full of life, love, and joy. But sometimes, they can be monsters. They leave the lights on and the milk out, put empty boxes of cereal back into the pantry, and pee on the toilet seat, all within five minutes. The list of how my children push me to insanity is endless.

The first time I tried the *Pause . . . What A Pleasure* exercise with my kids, they freaked out. They were doing something disruptive and annoying and I started to get angry, then quickly stopped and closed my eyes. I took a deep breath and said out loud as I slowly and deeply exhaled, "*Pause ... What A Pleasure.*"

My teenage daughter was disturbed, "What are you doing?" I shared with her how I was *Pausing* so I would not get reactive. I wanted to transform my anger into something positive. Once she realized I wasn't having a myocardial infarction, she relaxed and poked fun at me.

"You're doing what to what?" she asked again.

I explained that we have a choice when we encounter a *Life Problem*. We can either choose to get *Reactive*, which only creates more problems, or we can pause to get a handle on our emotions and change our negative response into something more positive.

Weeks passed before my children concocted a way to weaponize this new insight against me. One evening after dinner, while the kids were cleaning the kitchen and blaring loud music, I sensed the energy revving up and knew something was about to break.

My son was recklessly tossing ceramic dishes into the sink while joking with his siblings. I knew if I didn't step in, there would be a big mess to clean up. I turned down the music to calm the chaos and was about to speak but I was five seconds too late. My son tipped a wine glass onto the granite countertop before it rolled over the edge and crashed on the hardwood floor. The glass shattered into a million little sharp shards. There may be nothing I loathe more than cleaning up broken glass. Everyone spun around to see my reaction. Just as I was about to lash out at my son for his carelessness, he held up his hand and said, "Dad, remember pause . . . what a pleasure."

He was so proud of himself. The smile on his face was maniacal. He knew he had double trumped me. He broke a glass and got away with it. He also played me at my own game. I wanted to explode, but what was I supposed to do in that moment, get reactive and lose all credibility? Somewhere deep inside, I knew he was right. It's a glass. Glasses break. People make mistakes. I loved seeing my children laughing and playing together. A twenty dollar glass broke, so what?

My kids aren't psychopaths, but they seemed to receive pure joy from making their father lose his marbles. However, it didn't take me long to turn the tables that they had turned on me back on them and weaponize their weaponization!

Later, I stumbled onto a brilliant insight in a moment of reflection. Initially, I was attempting to teach them a different way of handling challenging situations by using words. They took my goodwill and turned it into a punchline of a joke. But I realized I had the last laugh because while they thought they were making me the butt of their innocent joking around, they were unaware of how I was teaching them how to use the *Pause ... What A Pleasure* tool through my actions which is a much more potent way of teaching anything.

Our relentless stream of reactive impulses will never totally subside. We are human. Things that are unfair happen to us unexpectedly, taking us by surprise. Practicing *Pause* when we are mildly triggered will give us the superpower to *Pause* in highly charged moments when we are stressed, exhausted, and overwhelmed.

There are plenty of opportunities in your daily life to practice *Pausing*. You walk outside to leave for a vacation and your car has a flat tire? *Pause* before you unleash a litany of expletives. You find out in a company-wide email the promotion you were promised was given to someone else. *Pause* and take a walk before speaking to anyone about your feelings. Your favorite team loses in the playoffs. Getting a little reactive here is okay as you cry in your beer. We all need somewhere to blow off steam. All of these incidents raise your blood pressure and disrupt your peace. But what if you chose to say, "*Pause ... What a pleasure*" instead?

The *Pause* is the sacred moment where you embrace your problems and step into your power. The *Pause* transforms your less mature, unhealthy self into a powerhouse of love, wisdom, and integrity. The *Pause* is the opportunity to put into practice all the wisdom you have learned from the many self-improvement books, podcasts, and therapy you have paid for over the years.

So what, exactly, is the pleasure of life's many annoying and hurtful experiences? Absolutely nothing. There is no pleasure in those terrible experiences. The satisfaction is knowing when these events happen, you get to transform your darkness (negativity) into the light (positivity).

This is the beginning of *The Transformational Path*. Everyday mundane experiences become sacred. This is how you grow and mature. This is what it looks like to take something difficult and learn about yourself through the experience. When you *Pause*, you are doing the work to take control of your life.

All this talk of embracing life's annoying or traumatizing moments might sound unnecessary or insensitive to those suffering terribly. This is a fair criticism. When someone is grieving, there are many ways to get it wrong and a few ways to get it right. I don't want anyone to feel like they have failed if they aren't able to say *Pause . . . What A Pleasure* when tragedy strikes. What I am suggesting takes time and practice. Remember, you have the power to choose how you go through an experience. The optimal time to hit the *Pause . . . What A Pleasure* button is as close to the onset of the situation as possible, but it doesn't need to happen at the beginning.

No one wants *Life Problems*, but the reality is they are inevitable. Taking our painful moments and transforming them through consciously choosing our path forward gives each experience meaning and purpose.

LISTEN TO YOURSELF

Reflect on today, or if it is the morning, reflect on yesterday. Take note of any interactions or situations when saying *Pause . . . What A Pleasure* would have been helpful. How did you respond? Were there any ramifications to how you reacted? Can you do anything now to make amends?

Think about how you would have liked to respond. Using the power of your imagination, act as a third party witnessing the interaction or experience and redo it by *Pausing* instead of overreacting.

You literally have to practice saying the words *Pause . . . What A Pleasure* before an actual triggering event happens or you will never be able to put this step into practice. The emotional energy of a difficult or negative situation is enormous. These events also trigger past emotions and unconscious responses we have used for years, maybe decades. To retrain yourself to say *Pause . . . What A Pleasure* is no different than going to the gym. It will take consistent hard work to see progress. Start practicing right now. Say *Pause . . . What A Pleasure* out loud right now. Notice how the words feel in your mouth. Notice what they feel like emotionally. Do you feel embarrassed to say the words? Why?

Next, seek out opportunities today to say *Pause . . . What A Pleasure.* Don't worry, you will have at least a dozen. Once you start looking for them they will pop up like weeds in a garden. Before long you will start to say it automatically for big and small things. In that moment congratulate yourself for transforming something ordinary into something sacred and by doing so you have practiced love, wisdom, and integrity.

18

STEP FIVE: THE WICKED LITTLE VOICE

If you have made it this far, you have crossed some challenging terrain on the way to summit your *Sacred Mountains*. Your next major test comes in the form of a loud-mouthed hater known as your *Inner Critic*. This slippery, self-saboteur manifests itself in many ways, but I prefer to call it what it is: a wicked little voice.

We all carry the potential for both greatness and self-destruction. Which destiny you choose is based on your actions. Your actions are formed out of the raw material of your thoughts. As stated earlier, what you think about you become.

You aren't responsible for what comes into your mind. You are responsible for what you allow to linger there. Any idea you think long enough will become a belief. Your beliefs are what you use to justify your actions. Think positive, optimistic, hopeful thoughts, good things happen. Think negative, cynical, hateful, selfish thoughts and bad things happen. It's a simple formula.

The wicked little voice is the architect of negative thoughts and bad ideas. This voice has no power over you beyond the power of suggestion, but few things are more powerful than an idea. This voice in your head cannot act independently in the physical world. You must take action on its behalf.

I am no expert on evil, but this little voice seems to possess evil qualities. It is sneaky. It hides its true intentions. It lies to you. It tells you things that cause harm to yourself and others. It is a double agent coming in the form of a friendly truth-teller but is your enemy hell-bent on your destruction. It tries to shame you. It isolates you and makes other people the enemy. What else would need to be added to this list to qualify it as evil?

As we discussed earlier, the potential to do evil resides in each of us. The seeds of good and evil are present in equal measure. I share this to empower you, not to discourage you. You must be aware of the power you possess to be able to wield it effectively.

If the seeds of evil are not nurtured, they go dormant. Remove all negative thoughts, love others, be generous and kind to others, do the deep work necessary to mature and heal your wounds, help others, do no harm, and be a safe person for those in your life. These are ways to starve those seeds of destruction while watering the seeds of love.

Our culture has a fascination with evil and darkness. It is preached from pulpits. We are obsessed with true crime T.V. shows, movies, and podcasts. However, the real evil you need to be most concerned about is an inside job. In other words, you are the evil you should most fear.

You can never rid yourself of this inner potential for evil. It is written into the D.N.A. of humanity. It can only be marginalized to the point of irrelevance and overcome with love. Nothing else will work. As John Steinbeck wrote, "All the goodness and the heroism will rise up again, then be cut down again and rise up. It isn't that the evil thing wins -- it never will -- but that it doesn't die."

Evil is complicated because most people don't fall easily into "good" or "evil." The same person who commits an evil act in one moment can turn around and do something very kind and generous in the next. How is this possible?

It is normal to crave the simplicity of a good black-and-white dichotomy. Good vs. Bad. Right vs. Wrong. Us vs. Them. Something or someone must be bad for us to be good. In this black-and-white universe, it is hard to comprehend how a police officer, for example, can be brave and heroic in one situation and in another commit crimes against individuals of a different race. Was this person deceiving us? Were they hiding their true identity? That is possible, but there is a more plausible explanation.

The more likely explanation is that while the officer has many good qualities, he allowed hateful, divisive thoughts to linger in his mind day after day, year after year. Maybe these thoughts weren't even his own. Perhaps they were part of his unspoken family belief system growing up. What if these were the beliefs held by the entire community where he lived? As a child, he had to conform to be accepted by the group. He was a child, what was he supposed to do? Maybe no one modeled love, wisdom, and integrity for him or showed him what it looks like to accept others who are different.

The crimes this man committed later in life were the natural consequences of letting that wicked little voice of evil go unchallenged. Yes, there are depraved psychopaths, but what is more common is a complicated mix of good and evil intentions in the average person. We are all susceptible to this weakness and must guard against it.

This is not a hopeless situation. You are not doomed to forever struggle against evil impulses. The solution is simple. St. Paul the Apostle wrote some simple instructions to his friends living in Rome about resisting their darker impulses, "Do not let evil defeat you; instead, conquer evil with good.[26]" It doesn't get much clearer than that.

In every situation, you have the potential to be courageous and heroic or cowardly and evil. If this is true, how do you choose good over evil? You must decide what you will do before you are tested. I constantly harped on my young players when I coached Little League baseball, "You play how you practice." How you respond in the critical moment of being tested determines how well you prepared before the test. The ancient Greek poet Archilochus summarized this idea in 660 BC, "We do not rise to the level of our expectations; we fall to the level of our training." If you do the work necessary to love yourself and others while cultivating an open, curious heart, you will find it much easier to have the integrity to resist evil impulses.

I acknowledge that using the example of a police officer and police brutality is a very sensitive and volatile issue in our culture. I considered replacing it with a less volatile subject but chose to leave it in because I think what it represents is a powerful dichotomy that is hard to reconcile. It is easy to understand how bad people do bad things but why do good people do bad things? We are all infected with the same virus but we also carry the cure within ourselves. Whatever side of this issue you plant your flag, the solution is the same. Those who seek justice and change in law enforcement and those who put their lives on the line every day to serve and protect have the common ground of love, wisdom, and integrity. Why not use these virtues as a foundation for growth, change, and forward progress?

Change is an unavoidable law of nature. No one stays the same. You will either progress or regress. How you change is determined by what you allow to linger in your mind day after day. As you do your work, you will gain the resilience to resist evil impulses and push away from that wicked little voice.

My advice for defeating the wicked little voice is to push away from it. Don't engage it. Don't entertain it. Don't listen to it. Don't argue with it. Just walk (or run) away.

Jocko Willink is a famous Navy SEAL. He is a hulking man, standing five feet eleven inches tall and weighing two hundred and thirty-five pounds. He has been trained by the best in the world to be a warrior. His advice regarding what to do if you find yourself in a situation that could turn into a fistfight is to run away. He reasons that you have no idea what might happen if you fight. The guy might have a knife or a gun or friends. If you can't get away, you fight; if you must fight, fight to kill. This is excellent advice for how to handle the wicked little voice.

When your wicked little voice starts to whisper those familiar insults about your body, levels harsh criticisms about your skills and abilities, or makes you feel hopeless, wondering why you are even alive, all you need to do is say with as little energy as possible, "No thank you." Push away from that destructive energy. In other words, your power to resist comes from maintaining control, not giving your power away.

It may seem like I contradict myself here but follow me for a moment. Eventually, you will learn how to use your negative thought energy to your benefit. For this to happen, the most essential quality you must possess is to authentically love yourself.

What this looks like in practice is to take the subject of the wicked little voice and turn the negative into something positive. The next chapter goes into greater detail about *The Voice of Love*. For now, an example may help you understand.

The wicked little voice is bland and basic, often repeating the same tired insults it has used for many years. There are a few general categories many people struggle with, including the body, loneliness, worthiness, and life purpose and direction.

If you hear the wicked little voice criticizing you in some way, you must take that negative energy and transform it into a positive statement about yourself. It may help to speak to yourself as if you were talking to a friend. If that wicked voice criticizes your physical appearance say, "Reb, you are a beautiful man. Reb, it is time to love yourself. Reb, you desire to be healthy and strong to fulfill your life plan. Reb, keep going! You are doing great! Reb, let's elevate your game and find exercises you enjoy. Let's eat healthy! Remember Reb, loving yourself is the most healthy thing you can do for your body."

One quick note when practicing positive, loving statements. You do not need to feel them for them to work. At first, all you need to do is say them. By speaking the truth over lies, you affirm your desire to live differently than you are living today. This is how everyone improves. We create a vision for who we want to be and how we want to live, then act in ways that bring that reality into existence. You are taking back your power by blocking the negative energy and replacing it with positive energy. The feelings will come later. The actions must come first.

Beware, there is always a risk going near that wicked little voice. This is why I initially recommend most people steer clear of it. When you feel ready, there is work for you to do. If/When you begin this work, do it with the help of others. Friends, family, and professionals are all great allies to have as you create a strong body and mind.

A side note: Other professionals may disagree with my assessment that the wicked little voice of evil is a fundamental aspect of human nature. They may resist the term "evil" because it sounds too religious. They may see this voice as an aspect of the human mind that needs to be redeemed to live a healthy life and not something to be shunned. I respect that position and believe it holds merit. My observation is that many people are tortured by their wicked little voice. I want to give people practical tools to help them alleviate as much unnecessary suffering as possible. Richard Schwartz, the founder of Internal Family Systems, has a book called *No Bad Parts.* I agree with his assessment. All of the many parts a person has are good and worthy. You don't need to demonize any part of yourself. I see the wicked little voice not as a psychological part but as a spiritual state fundamental to every human being that cannot be redeemed or eliminated so it must be tolerated. It is there as a test and the test is to resist it, not give into it. However, you can minimize this inner evil to the point of irrelevance by focusing on being the most loving, compassionate person toward yourself and others.

Here is a quick assessment to determine your mental and spiritual health. It only takes a moment and you can do this throughout the day. All you need to do is reflect on the quality of your inner dialogue. What does the voice in your head sound like as you go about your day? If you make a mistake is it harsh or kind? Neutral or hateful? Funny or critical? Does it always look for what's wrong, or can it see the good in every situation? What type of language does that voice in your head use? What is the tone of the voice? Does the critical voice you hear sound like anyone from your past? Your inner dialogue is a perfect tool to measure the health of your inner life.

Remember, you are not responsible for what comes into your mind. You are only responsible for what you allow to linger there. You have the power to choose your inner dialogue. You are not a helpless victim standing by without any control. If changing this voice feels beyond your control right now, take heart, all you need is more practice. Be patient with yourself. Do not criticize yourself while learning this new skill. Be aware that the wicked little voice will see a blank mind as an opportunity to fill it with negative, self-critical energy. Its biggest weapons are doubt and fear. You can replace doubt and fear with love and courage.

LISTEN TO YOURSELF

Pay attention to your internal dialogue throughout the day today. Notice the words you use and the tone of voice. It will be more effective if you can jot the mood of your inner dialogue as it happens. Make a note on your phone for later reflection in your *Sacred Space* time. Try to find words that describe the overall tone of the voice. Some examples might be supportive, neutral, acerbic, demeaning, or demanding.

How do you talk to yourself in different situations? Do the words you use or tone of voice change under stress? Is the voice your voice or someone you know? Are you constantly apologizing unnecessarily? Do you insult your body or your intellect by making jokes about yourself? Ask people you know well what their inner dialogue is like.

19

STEP SIX: THE VOICE OF LOVE

How you talk to yourself matters. Even if you resist the wicked little voice, you will eventually return to your old negative habits if you don't replace them with something positive. As mentioned, *The Voice of Love* is the only thing powerful enough to displace that wicked little voice.

The Voice of Love is something anyone can cultivate. This is done by paying attention to your internal dialogue and adjusting as necessary. Noticing the subtle shifts in the tone of your inner voice from positive or neutral to negative will reveal areas that need attention.

The Transformational Path is a process of reprogramming yourself to respond differently to stress giving you clear instructions that lead to inner peace. The first opportunity to change the arc of a difficult experience is the *Pause . . . What A Pleasure* moment. The second opportunity comes when you reject all the negativity hurled at you by the wicked little voice. The third opportunity comes when you replace the cynicism with *The Voice of Love.* This is how you retrain your brain to work for you and not against you.

In his seminal work on trauma and healing, Bessel van der Kolk notes that our bodies keep the score, meaning it stores our experiences as body memories. That is true for trauma, but it is also true for love. Every step toward loving yourself in thoughts, words, and actions registers in your body and moves you closer to inner peace.

The Voice of Love is the playful, fun part of *The Transformational Path*. There aren't any rules for how to love yourself, so get creative with the things that light you up. *The Voice of Love* is not just how you speak to yourself but also what you do for yourself. For some that might be something as simple as sitting at a coffee shop reading a book. For others it might be riding a dune buggy in the desert before jumping out of an airplane. Celebrate who you are and you'll be loving yourself.

In addition to being fun, The *Voice of Love* has the power to heal. You cannot heal and move forward if you haven't forgiven yourself. *The Voice of Love* supports you as you do the work necessary to correct past mistakes and heal emotional wounds. *The Voice of Love* is the tool to create a positive vibe that will enrich your life.

The Voice of Love may begin as something you do as part of *The Transformational Path*, but it is so much more. You want *The Voice of Love* to be a way of life. What does it mean for *The Voice of Love* to be a way of life? It means transforming as many experiences as possible into opportunities to love yourself and others.

If you are wondering what *The Voice of Love* looks like in the real world, here is an example. I created this exercise to help me when I am having one of those days where I feel depressed, lonely, or sad and can't seem to shake it. I call it the *I Know This To Be True* exercise. The instructions are simple.

The first step is to connect to your body by placing your hand on your heart and taking three, slow breaths. Give yourself a moment to relax. The second step is to close your eyes and repeat out loud, "I know this to be true," followed by a truthful statement of gratitude. For example, you might say, "I know this to be true . . . my children love me. I know this to be true . . . my body is healthy and strong. I know this to be true . . . I love my work. I know this to be true . . . I am living my life dedicated to the virtues of love, wisdom, and integrity." Repeat this until you begin to feel better.

This simple but effective exercise engages the body, emotions, and mind by reminding you of all the beautiful things in your life. I have never done this exercise and come away feeling worse. It helps me navigate the choppy waters of overwhelming emotions. It is also effective for stopping a negative thought loop.

I want you to become a master at stopping all negative thoughts and replacing them with loving, grateful, generous, powerful thoughts. This skill rewires your body and brain to eradicate old patterns of negativity and elevate your view of yourself.

Here is a short review of what we have covered so far. You encounter a *Life Problem*, big or small, and at the moment you want to get reactive, you have a choice to make. You can get emotionally reactive, you can run away and avoid the problem, or you can say, "*Pause . . . What A Pleasure.*" The *Pause* quiets the storm, preventing whatever bad thing just happened from turning into a worse situation. As soon as you find the heroic courage to restrain yourself, you will be confronted with that wicked little voice hell-bent on your destruction. Now is the time to go inward and harness the power to push away from the negative voice and embrace your inner *Voice of Love*. Once you have accomplished this, you can take the love you have shown yourself and shine that light outwards toward others.

LISTEN TO YOURSELF

Seek to cultivate a robust treasure trove of positive, truthful thoughts about yourself to replace what that wicked little voice tells you. Use the second-person point of view. Here are examples of present-moment statements:

- *You love your job and you are doing great. Keep going!*
- *You are a wonderful mother/father. You are giving your children a great gift of love.*
- *You have done the work and have a healthy, strong body.*

Here are examples of future-oriented aspirational statements:

- *(For someone who wants to lose weight) You are healthy and getting healthier every day.*
- *(For someone starting a business or new job) You are working hard to build your business. Keep going! Push yourself to achieve your goals.*

These are only examples to get your creativity flowing. Make statements that are personal to you and your situation. Write them in your journal so you can return to them often when you are struggling through a difficult time.

20

STEP SEVEN: GENEROSITY

Each step of *The Transformational Path* carries energy. The energy of *Generosity* transforms you first, then the world around you, by infusing it with the vitality of giving. Every time you practice *Generosity*, you positively impact the world. *Generosity* is helping others, but it is ultimately about helping yourself by utilizing personal sacrifice for others as the vehicle for your personal transformation.

The quality of your thoughts determines whether you are a creator or a destroyer. What you do with your thoughts is what you do with your life. You may recognize a theme emerging throughout *The Transformational Path* of the power of your mind to transform your reality.

As you engage the never-ending waterfall of your thoughts, you become an active participant in your life, not a passive observer. The active participant approach acknowledges your power to shape the world around you. The active participant approach sees each thought as a small unit of energy connected to a vast constellation of energy you call your mind.

Generosity is such a powerful tool in *The Transformational Path* because of the sheer number of opportunities you have in a single day to practice this step. One way to practice *Generosity* is through "May you" blessings. If someone cuts you off in traffic, first say, "Pause . . . What A Pleasure!" then follow it up with, "May you arrive at your destination safely." If you see a homeless person, send some love their way, "May you find food and shelter today" then slide them five dollars. If someone you love is hurting, say a blessing of healing for them, "May you be comforted today," then take them French bread and soup.

When I pass a stranger, I often silently toss a blessing in their direction. Each blessing takes only a few seconds of my time. There are not many things you can do in such a short time that can have such a positive impact.

Dear Reader, may you be blessed today with joy, love, and prosperity. May you know that you are loved. May you see your beauty both inward and outward. May you be successful in your work. May you be blessed with abundance.

LISTEN TO YOURSELF

Start today expressing *Generosity* toward others by sending them silent blessings. Try and find a group of people that you normally judge and send them a blessing instead. Do it wherever you are and whatever you are doing. You don't have to know the person or be in the same physical space with them. Send a blessing to someone you love, wherever they may be. Here are examples:

- *(When you see someone jogging in your neighborhood) May you be healthy.*
- *(When you see someone of a different race or gender) May you feel at peace today. May you know that you are loved today. May you feel safe today.*
- *(For anybody) May you have a beautiful day.*

21

STEP EIGHT: SACRED SPACE

Sacred Space is not one thing, one exercise, one practice. It is a way of living that seeks to make the ordinary extraordinary by transforming the mundane into something sacred. However, for the purpose of illustration let's define *Sacred Space* as a time set aside each day to connect with your intuitive wisdom.

I call this time of reflection and listening *Sacred Space* because it is set apart from the rest of your day. What makes this daily exercise sacred? Your intention is what infuses anything you do with meaning. A sip of red wine becomes the blood of Jesus Christ. Eggs, flour, butter, and sugar become a cake to celebrate a milestone in life. A piece of metal dug out of the earth symbolizes eternal love.

So many people feel they are simply cogs in the wheel of life. They believe what they do every day makes no difference. People yearn for their life to matter. They want to feel what they are doing has a bigger purpose that positively impacts the world. When you strive to live each day with love, wisdom, and integrity, you are making the world a better place one moment at a time. Mother Teresa once said, "We cannot do great things. We can only do small things with great love."

I am here to remind you that your life matters. What you do matters. What you think matters. What you say matters. Giving your life meaning starts with taking control of the only thing in this world you can control, which is yourself.

Becoming the best possible version of yourself while creating the best possible reality is the quickest way to infuse your life with meaning. When you are at peace, successful, healed, and whole, you also want that for others, so you share more of yourself. You open your heart to others. You become the opposite of narcissistic. You become altruistic. A practical way to do this kind of work is by creating your own *Sacred Space* at the beginning of each day.

Mornings are optimal for *Sacred Space*. There is an ephemeral energy at the beginning of the day that is full of possibilities. You are as rested in the morning as you will be all day. Buddhists teach that you can always begin again, and there is no better time to hit the reset button than at the start of a new day. Today might be when you meet your soulmate, get a promotion, or decide to start your own business. The stillness of the early morning is unlike any other time of day.

All you need to create a *Sacred Space* is yourself and an intention to go inward and reflect on your life. A pen and a journal are helpful, especially when starting out, as they provide a focus for your wandering attention. As you settle into these early morning rituals, you may find using a meditation app on your phone or tablet beneficial. Be careful with electronic devices because the incessant chiming and vibrating can lure you away from your peaceful silence and into the world of busyness.

Feel free to add whatever fosters a sense of creativity and inspiration. You could keep a yoga mat nearby for stretching. You might want to include candles, books, icons, totems, prayer beads, poetry books, a Bible or other religious materials, art, photographs, precious stones, coffee, tea, etc. but don't let planning your space prevent you from getting started. One of the first tests you will face is how much you procrastinate before getting started.

You have begun your *Sacred Space* practice, now what? Great question! Anything you want. Own the time. Make it yours. However, I have learned that many people struggle with such broad instructions. A little guidance here might go a long way.

Remember, the purpose of this time is to pause, go inward, and listen. If you are experiencing a *Life Problem*, then it makes sense to focus on that issue. Begin by asking exploratory questions. What emotional impact has this problem had on me? Are there any valuable lessons I have learned from the problem so far? What hard truths have I had to acknowledge about myself? What obstacles are blocking me from resolving this problem? As you write your answers, it can feel like work. You think. You write. You think some more. You write some more. If you stay with this process long enough a transition occurs. The effort you are putting into thinking and writing shifts from work to a flow state. Ideas begin to emerge with less effort. Solutions you have never considered start to form. This might sound like hyperbole but I have experienced this so many times. It doesn't happen every time but based on my experience it happens more often than not and the quality of what comes through is very high.

The best way to manifest your future is to be clear about what you want your future to be and take steps toward making it a reality. In your *Sacred Space* time your imagination to visualize yourself achieving those milestones. Although this rehearsal is only in your imagination, your brain has a hard time differentiating a mind movie from reality. Either way you will create neural pathways that create the right mental environment for advancement.

An example of this might be asking for a raise. You could begin by rehearsing everything from getting dressed, driving to work, walking into your supervisor's office, asking for a raise, and driving home feeling proud of yourself for being courageous. You could practice different ways to word your request and prepare yourself for responses to each one. You could craft a plan for how to respond if you are given the runaround.

If your life is going well, fantastic. Keep doing what you're doing. Use your *Sacred Space* time to build up your resilience so that you will be prepared when the blue skies turn dark. The obvious benefit of things going well is that you aren't in a crisis. Instead of putting out fires and being overwhelmed by stress, you get to dream. Don't waste this window of opportunity. Do you want a new house, a rental property, or a cottage on the beach? Would collecting art inspire you? Should you train for an Iron Man marathon? What would it take for you to become an EDM deejay and perform at Bonnaroo? All of these ideas must start in your mind before they become a plan which leads to actions that become your reality.

I am adamant that journaling needs to be part of your *Sacred Space* routine. Journaling might include writing long prose, but it could also be jotting down a few notes on what comes up for you. Why am I so adamant? Journaling is a therapeutic tool, like therapy, yoga, or meditation. Something happens when you think and write that doesn't happen when you just think. You forget things. You fail to make connections. You get distracted and lose momentum. Research by James W. Pennebaker[27] has shown the many health benefits of therapeutic writing.

Another benefit of journaling is having a written record of your experiences you can review at a later time. You think you will remember that inspiring idea for a song, the details of a new business opportunity, or a solution to a long-standing problem, but you won't. They will vanish. Trust me on this one, write it down.

Committing to journaling right now doesn't mean you must journal every day for the rest of your life. Just do it for a month and see what comes up. If you write half of the days, that is a huge accomplishment. Novel insights into problems and creative ideas will be your reward. Journaling gives you access to your unconscious mind and as Carl Jung wrote, "Until you make the unconscious conscious, it will direct your life and you will call it fate."

Processing your thoughts, dreams, hopes, desires, fears, and emotions will bring insights, comfort, A-ha moments, truth, and healing, though you may go through some challenging moments if you are processing past traumatic experiences. As you make progress, fewer stress hormones, such as epinephrine (adrenalin), cortisol, and norepinephrine will circulate through your body. Instead, you will bathe your body and brain with life-enhancing chemicals such as dopamine, serotonin, oxytocin, and endorphins.

Once, I had a client who had a very difficult childhood. She continued to experience trauma into adulthood. She struggled to keep it together in one session and eventually broke down in tears. She had recently lost her husband and was having difficulty completing all the new tasks her new reality required.

I listened patiently and when she finished, I took time to reframe what she said to reflect the truth of her situation. She paused and then reached for her journal. She flipped through several pages until she found the entry she was looking for. She told me she had written those exact words to herself the night before. My words were her words that ended up being just the healing words she needed to hear. What was so interesting was that she had forgotten she wrote those things to herself until I reminded her. That is a powerful example of journaling in real life. The truth you need to hear is within you.

When it comes to journaling, if you wrote, "I don't know what to write," for three pages, you would have accomplished something worthwhile. Why? Because there is no magic formula for unlocking the solutions to your problems. There is just the work and remember you must keep doing the work because the work never ends. Journaling is good, honest work.

LISTEN TO YOURSELF

Plan where you want your *Sacred Space* to be and when you plan to do it. Do this ahead of time and tidy up the area. Fold any blankets. Remove any trash. Make sure the light bulbs in the lamps work. Bring in a candle and some matches. Remove any excess materials that could be distracting. Keep your journal and pen in this spot so you don't have to go searching for it in the morning. Only do this if you can be assured of privacy. Otherwise, keep your journal entries on an electronic device you can lock with a passcode. Set reminders on your phone and block out the time on your work and personal calendars. Commit to this practice for a month. If you need to get up earlier than you typically wake, set an alarm. Acknowledge that this is going to be difficult in the beginning to prepare yourself for the resistance.

22

STEP NINE: STAND GUARD

When the phrase *Stand Guard* first came to mind, I immediately thought of the Proverb from King Solomon, *"Guard your heart above all else for it determines the course of your life.*[28]*"*

Guard your heart. Guard your heart. Your heart determines the course of your life.

What a powerful idea. What does it mean?

Another image that came to mind was a soldier keeping watch on the wall. In high school, I took a senior trip to New York City for a conference on Wall Street. One of the planned activities for us was the Broadway show *A Few Good Men.* I will never forget the experience of seeing Col. Jessup on stage talking about soldiers standing on a wall guarding our freedoms, *"We use words like honor, code, loyalty. We use these words as the backbone of a life defending something."*

I think of the sentinels watching the *Tomb of the Unknown Soldier.* I think of the courage of *Tank Man,* the name given to the unidentified man who stood in front of a column of tanks in Tiananmen Square in China.

At the core of *Standing Guard* are the virtues of love, wisdom, and integrity. It is in the *Standing Guard* that these virtues are practiced in the real world.

When you think of *Love*, don't think in broad, ethereal terms. Think about the grittier side of life. Think about what it means for you to love when loving gets hard. Think about what it means to love yourself. What does it mean to love friends and family you disagree with? What does it mean to love those who hate who you are or what you stand for?

How do you *Stand Guard?* Commit to studying and practicing the virtues of love, wisdom, and integrity every day. The more you practice, the better prepared you will be when the inevitable tests come your way. It is difficult, and sometimes impossible, to know who or what will bring you challenges. Whoever or whatever it may be, they will most likely take you by surprise. *Standing Guard* is the best way to be prepared for whatever comes.

Embracing the paths of love, wisdom, and integrity will protect you from many avoidable dangers. It offers those you love the protection that only your integrity can offer. A man with integrity is a man in his power. The virtues cannot protect you from every hardship, but they can save you from many, if not most, of them.

The protection gained from living a life dedicated to love, wisdom, and integrity goes even further. When you *Stand Guard*, you are protecting friends, your friend's marriage and their children. You are protecting your business and your business partners. If you are an athlete, you are protecting the whole team. If you are an actor, writer, or musician you are protecting the crew, the investors, the band, the companies that are investing in your success. If you are a politician, you are protecting those who elected you. There is not a group, business, organization, or family that couldn't benefit from practicing love, wisdom, and integrity. By *Standing Guard,* you bring peace to your community, protecting those you may never meet.

Imagine the ripple effect of just one action you take that is moti-
vated by love, wisdom, and integrity. Now, imagine the power of a
group of people in your community choosing to live these virtues. By
Standing Guard, you are harnessing your power to love those around
you and positively transform your life and the life of others.

When it comes to *Standing Guard,* integrity is the virtue out front.
It takes courage to make the right decision when it is easier to make
the wrong one. It takes courage to keep doing the work when life
isn't working. Integrity means holding yourself accountable to your
own greatness and not getting distracted by temporary circumstances.
Greatness already exists within you. It is just waiting for you to
activate it!

If you have yet to achieve your version of personal greatness, don't
worry, it's not too late. It is always there waiting for you. If you are
reading these words, you still have time. Committing to live each day
with love, wisdom, and integrity is the most direct path to unleashing
your greatness. The closest you, or any of us, will ever come to having
superpowers is by *Standing Guard* at the door of your heart, mind, and
body with love, wisdom, and integrity.

Standing Guard requires a strong mind but it requires more than a
strong mind. Your mind is a formidable weapon but it has its limitations. In addition to your mind you need emotional intelligence and
body awareness.

Emotional awareness comes in the form of being connected to your
heart so you can better understand the inner landscape of your emotions. Thoughts and ideas are the language of the mind while emotions
and sensations are the language of the body. Each has their own type of
wisdom and provides unique insights. On their own they each possess
power but they are much more powerful when used in unison with
one another. The mind without body awareness and emotions is sterile
and cold. Emotions and bodily sensations without logic are erratic and
prone to exaggeration.

Most people, especially men, are far more comfortable operating with their logical mind. A part of this can be attributed to biology but the majority is due to a lack of appreciation for and understanding of the intelligence of the body and emotions. The key to incorporating the body and emotions with the mind is to embrace experiences as they come to you in the way they come to you. If your muscles are tense, there is a pit in your stomach, or your hands are shaking, those are all messages for you to decode.

When you are feeling sad, depressed, and lonely, if you push those emotions away they will leave. You have that power. But what if you embraced them and allowed them to teach you more about yourself? That could possibly eliminate the stress your body is holding by creating a safe space for all of you to show up.

In truth, my hope is that you come to see your whole life as a *Sacred Space* waiting for you to take advantage of the immense power you hold. By combining your logical brain, your emotional life, and awareness of bodily sensations with love, wisdom, and integrity, you are receiving valuable information necessary to make the most informed, wisest decisions possible. This is what it means to *Stand Guard* at the door of your heart, mind, and body with love, wisdom, and integrity.

Many people secretly live with shame because of things they have said or done in the past. While shame is like battery acid on your soul, it can, under rare circumstances, have a positive influence. Shame can be a safeguard by preventing you from repeating the behaviors that made you feel ashamed. The problem with using shame in this way is its terrible side effects. Think of one of those pharmaceutical commercials you see during the evening news. The list of possible side effects is remarkably long. The list is equally long for using shame to punish yourself for previous self-destructive behaviors. The commercial for shame might sound something like this, "*When shaming yourself, you may experience the following side effects. Low self-esteem. Social isolation. Self-loathing. Closing down of your heart toward others. You may experience abnormal behaviors such as bouts of anger or depression. Thoughts of worthlessness have been reported. Call a therapist or friend if you develop thoughts of harming yourself. If you are already depressed, you may experience worsening symptoms. Alcohol may increase these symptoms. Side effects may also include increased stress, a decline in the function of your immune system, and abnormal weight gain or loss. Shame is not for everyone, but if you decide to use it, we're absolutely almost positive you will be fine."*

If you feel shame for something from your past, you can start to heal this by allowing integrity to take its place right now in the present moment. Committing to acting with integrity enables you to own your part in what happened in the past but not remain imprisoned there.

Love, wisdom, and integrity will prevent you from returning to those self-destructive thoughts and unhealthy behaviors. This is what will prevent you from making the same mistakes over and over. Those who do not commit to living with love, wisdom, and integrity will not have a plan for how to withstand their darker impulses. They will inevitably fail themselves and continue hurting those they care about the most.

LISTEN TO YOURSELF

Read the following commitment and ask yourself if you are ready to *Stand Guard* at the door of your heart, mind and body by living *The Sacred Life*. If you are, make the following commitment to yourself:

I commit to keep doing the work because the work never ends. The work is to grow in love, wisdom, and integrity and to help others grow in love, wisdom, and integrity.

23

STEP TEN: MAX EFFORT

As my kids grew older and left the safety of our home to start school, I fell into the same trap as so many other modern-day parents. I wanted to boost my children's confidence so they would believe they could do anything and be anything. According to the research[29], the mistake I made was praising their innate talent and intelligence, which are fixed and outside of their control, and not their effort, which *is* in their control.

At some point, every child encounters a new concept they have yet to learn. This is how their minds grow. They struggle to solve the problem and feel frustrated until they learn the new concept but more importantly learn how to learn. Suppose the child was continually praised for their intelligence, yet they need help to solve a problem. In that case, the research indicates those praised for their intelligence begin to doubt their abilities, resulting in waning effort or giving up entirely.

The result is that this pattern leaves smart kids feeling dumb and talented kids with zero motivation. They often quit if they don't get it on the first try. Why? They have no control over their naturally given intelligence, so what's the point in trying? They created the narrative that more effort won't make a difference if they don't understand it. It's not all bad news for parents. What children, as well as adults, need praise for and do have control over is their effort.

The same is true for *The Transformational Path*. You choose how much or how little effort you invest in each step. When you encounter a *Life Problem* you don't know how to solve, do you react negatively by getting angry or avoiding the problem altogether? Both reactions require a tremendous effort, but it's an effort in the wrong direction of *Reactive Behaviors*. It is in the direction of hiding from yourself or others. These negative behaviors recycle you into old patterns, causing more negative reactions.

Each step of *The Transformational Path* offers opportunities for you to give your *Max Effort* when tackling difficult challenges. When you *Pause*, you are applying a positive effort toward restraining your desire to act out in negative, harmful ways. Pushing away from your *Inner Critic* and moving toward *The Voice of Love* is giving your *Max Effort* to breathe life into a situation instead of chaos. When you are *Generous*, practicing your *Sacred Space,* and *Standing Guard*, you are making heroic efforts to overcome your weaknesses so you can funnel your energy into achieving personal greatness.

The ultimate gift of giving your *Max Effort* is a clear conscience, knowing you did all you could do. That is why it is the next to last step in *The Transformational Path* before achieving *Inner Peace*. Even when things don't work out as desired or expected, you can feel confident you have given your *Max Effort.* You can surrender and let what will unfold do so in its own way and in its own time.

A word of caution regarding *Max Effort.* Some people will get wrapped around the axle trying to figure out precisely what *Max Effort* means in every situation. It can turn into a time-wasting ambiguous effort in pursuit of perfection that can never be achieved. By getting lost in yet another rabbit hole of perfection, people can hide from themselves while convincing themselves they are doing the work. In reality they are avoiding the real work that needs to be done. Avoiding work by doing unnecessary work is a great way to hide from the hard work that is most important.

Rather than thinking of *Max Effort* as an exact, precise measurement, think of it more as a general sense of a job well done. Does the job feel complete? Do you feel you gave your best effort given the limitations of your situation? Do you feel at peace about your effort? Why? Why not? If you reflect and feel you didn't give your *Max Effort,* take the experience to your *Sacred Space* time and explore what happened and how you can do better next time. Don't beat yourself up about it. Learn from it, change, and let it be a constructive rather than destructive experience.

LISTEN TO YOURSELF

Conduct an honest assessment of your life to determine if you are giving *Max Effort* in every area. Do this for each relationship, your work, and yourself. Remember that *Max Effort* does not mean giving 100% all the time. That is a recipe for burnout. Sometimes *Max Effort* is 20% or 5%. Remind yourself often that giving too much of yourself is not *Max Effort.* Overextending yourself is a *Reactive Behavior* fueled by trying to get your needs met in an unhealthy way. This self-destructive cycle always leads to exhaustion, resentment, and setbacks.

Do not fall into the trap of thinking *Max Effort* means you have to continually exhaust yourself for the sake of others. *Max Effort* might tire you out in the moment, but this type of fatigue is temporary and should bring peace, harmony, and balance to your life. If it doesn't, then you are overextending yourself and a painful correction will be needed until you *Pause*, reset, and rebalance yourself. If you do that, then you just time traveled and solved a problem before it happened and saved yourself a lot of unnecessary suffering.

24

THE SACRED LIFE

The Sacred Life is a way of life guided by the virtues of love, wisdom, and integrity. This life is rooted in compassion, curiosity, and courage and lived out each day through the body, felt in the emotions, and directed by thoughts. To live *The Sacred Life* we must have compassion for ourselves to authentically extend compassion to others. We must be curious about ourselves, others, and the world around us or we risk being frozen in time preventing any growth. Finally, to act with courage means doing the next right thing no matter the personal sacrifice required.

You need not join our group, pay any dues, or pledge an allegiance to anyone other than yourself to live *The Sacred Life*. All you need to do is make the following commitment to yourself: *I commit to keep doing the work because the work never ends. The work is to grow in love, wisdom, and integrity and to help others grow in love, wisdom, and integrity.*

Each person's individual work is unique to their story and circumstances. Your work will not look like mine and mine will not look like yours. When you start to do your work the first test you will face will be the urge to quit. Like meditation or creating a *Sacred Space* you may start out strong but soon the new energy will fade and you'll be left with a choice. Do you continue even though you don't feel like it and you're not seeing much, if any, progress or do you embrace the suck and keep moving forward?

In the beginning, the work you have to do is the hardest because there is most likely a backlog of problems you have failed to address. I can guarantee that as you do the work the problems you must solve get incrementally better, then a little better. Over time this acts like compounding interest and begins to show big dividends. I call these better problems and I explain them using this analogy. Bad problems are things like not being able to pay the rent and buy groceries. Better problems would be like going on vacation and having to decide if you want to go to the hotel pool and sip Margaritas or head to the beach and swim in the ocean. The formula is simple. The more work you do, the better your problems. That is another reward for doing the work.

Although you do not need to join our community to live *The Sacred Life* I hope you do! My mission is to change the world one man at a time by bringing the virtues of love, wisdom, and integrity into every arena of life. This includes business, education, sports, religion, politics, law enforcement, the arts, medicine, families, marriages, and parenting to name but a few. I want to create a place where men and women can find romantic partners who align with love, wisdom, and integrity. I want employers to find quality employees that align with love, wisdom, and integrity. I want investors to be able to invest in companies led by men and women whose values are aligned with love, wisdom, and integrity. I envision a community that confidently refers clients and customers to one another because they know they can trust a business that operates with love, wisdom, and integrity as part of its core philosophy. I invite you to be part of that change bringing your unique skills and desires to the community.

I call this *Book One* because I envision many more books being written not only by me, but by our community on an expanded array of topics. The vision for *Book Two* is to chronicle your stories of how listening to yourself and loving yourself have transformed your life. If you have a story about how *The Transformational Path* has benefited you please share. Send your stories to stories@sacredlife.co.

Living an ordinary life takes little conscious effort. You do whatever needs to be done and when that is complete you mindlessly move on to the next thing. *The Sacred Life* is a choice. It is a commitment to yourself to live with intention.

The Sacred Life protects you against poor judgment and bad decisions. We all make mistakes. We all need forgiveness. We all need a plan to learn from our mistakes and avoid making them again. Living each day with love, wisdom, and integrity is the best possible plan to prevent future lapses in judgment.

When life is good, people convince themselves that what they are doing is working and nothing needs to change. All the evidence points to that logical conclusion. However, when someone is acting in ways that harm themselves or others, their success gives them a false sense of security blinding them from the dangers of their actions. Eventually their lack of integrity will be exposed and a reckoning required. The reason love, wisdom, and integrity are so powerful is that they give you a code to live by in good and bad times and a plan for how to solve life's most perplexing problems.

PART THREE

25

CASE STUDIES

A case study offers in-depth explanations of abstract, theoretical ideas in the context of real world experiences. In the following case studies, I attempt to illustrate what the step-by-step process of listening to yourself can look like via my own personal stories.

One of the biggest obstacles to overcome when learning to listen to yourself is how simple the practice appears on the surface yet how complex the lived experience feels in the moment. It can be hard to know whether you are doing it right during a difficult situation yet seem so straightforward and clear after the fact.

The subject matter of my experiences fall outside mainstream religion and traditional psychology. I chose these topics for case studies for several reasons. First, this is what happened to me as I practiced listening to myself. My personal experiences offer me the authenticity to speak from a first-person perspective. I am not creating a Frankensteinian fictionalized narrative stitched together from other people's stories. These are my stories and my experiences.

Another reason I chose these subjects is simple, these are the stories I had to draw from. I had no preset agenda for my inner explorations post-divorce. I was desperate for relief from my overwhelming pain and followed whatever clues presented themselves. From that vulnerable place these are the stories that emerged.

The topics covered in these case studies live on the wild, untamed edges of human experience. By sharing these experiences with you I am not suggesting you should take psilocybin or change your religious beliefs about what happens when you die. This is not a university textbook claiming facts nor a religious document trying to persuade you to adopt a particular belief. The point is not to change your mind on these subjects but to illustrate how to listen to yourself on a deep level.

Let's face it, we love to be entertained. These stories are as much for entertainment as they are illustrations. What better way to entertain you than venturing into areas of life most people will never experience. Our brains crave the thrill of novelty and the safety of living vicariously through other people's experiences.

I entered each experience as both an active participant and skeptical observer. The primary problem with inquiries into the field of psychedelics and parapsychology is that the subject's experiences are highly personal and ultimately unprovable. No one will ever be able to convince me that during my psilocybin experience my soul didn't leave this earthly plane and travel to another dimension. However, I cannot prove to you or anyone else that I, in fact, did leave this dimension. However, that does not leave us without any evidence even if it is only the secondary effects. A friend once told me that if the process of healing doesn't lead to more love, it wasn't an authentic experience. Each of the following experiences led me to a greater love for myself and to loving others in a deeper, more authentic way. That is all I need for these experiences to be authentic to me. It is my hope that your listening experiences lead you to a deeper love for yourself and others.

A problematic issue that these controversial areas of spirituality have to contend with is their void of accountability. Anyone with a notion to be a spiritual teacher can buy a pack of tarot cards and dowsing pendulum and call themselves a psychic. As of this writing *The Windbridge Institute*[30], one of the few facilities in the United States that conducts actual scientifically based research on psychic medium abilities, has depleted their funding and paused further research on the subject. The lack of accountability in this field means that many with mental illness and those with narcissistic disposition will be drawn to the easy access, power over others, and the ability to make a decent living from grieving and desperate people. There are many cases of fraudulent psychic mediums. However, the same could be said for politicians and preachers. The problem isn't psychic mediums or politicians as much as it is our fragile humanity being constantly tempted to give into our darker impulses of greed, jealousy, and fear.

When it comes to what has been most helpful to me practically and spiritually to live a virtuous life, it was neither my religious upbringing nor my psychological training that provided me the tools I needed. It was a direct, real life encounter with God that transformed an ordinary walk in the park into something extraordinary. The day I received the directive to live my life according to the virtues of love, wisdom, and integrity was nothing less than a miraculous, transformational *Road To Damascus* experience. I do want to mention that I use the name God here with great trepidation. I know this term is triggering for many who have experienced trauma from religious institutions and those claiming to speak for God. I only use it for the sake of simplicity and to avoid confusion. I use the name God as a symbol for all things spiritually available to us earth-bound souls.

Everyday since hearing the message on my walk, I have tried my very best to live according to those eternal virtues. It is my deepest desire that I never get off the path again but if I do, I now have a plan to follow to guide me back to safety. Because of my experience, I now know what it means to love myself and listen to myself. I know who I am. I know what I believe. I know that everyone can benefit by living with love, wisdom, and integrity.

Christians often use the term "fruits"[31] of a person's life as the standard by which they can be judged. In practice, my spiritual life is more active now than ever before. I pray more frequently. I seek to live a simple life free of unnecessary conflict. I am kinder to myself and practice generosity toward others. I do not say these things to elevate myself but to point to the power of love, wisdom, and integrity to transform lives.

The subjects of death, dying and what comes next fascinates all of us because we are all headed down the one way street called life on Earth. I don't believe our essence ultimately dies, but that provides little comfort as our mortal bodies march toward inevitable annihilation. I think more people should get out of their comfort zones and go on spiritual quests. Any spirituality trapped behind the prison walls of fear is limited and potentially harmful. As John the Evangelist wrote, "There is no fear in love; perfect love drives out all fear. So then, love has not been made perfect in anyone who is afraid, because fear has to do with punishment."[32]

I am not surprised that my journey led me to forbidden territory on the outskirts of socially acceptable spirituality. I tend toward the bizarre, the weird, the out of the way locations. As an example of my peculiar proclivity, Atlas Obscura is a website that bills itself as "The Definitive Guide To The World's Hidden Wonders". I use it to find quirky local attractions in new cities. I suggest you check it out as well. My curiosity for the uncommon explains my affinity for and comfortability with unique experiences. I am drawn to strange people, strange places, and strange experiences. I read books most people don't read and watch TV shows most people don't watch. Have you ever seen the television show *John From Cincinnati*?

The roads leading up a mountain are never straight. They wind around corners switching back and forth with every turn. It is impossible to see what lies around the next turn until you get there. My stories offer practical examples of what it will look like for you to listen to yourself and follow your curiosity. If you must know what's going to happen before you get to a bend in the road, you probably won't get very far.

26

CASE STUDY #1: WHAT HAPPENS WHEN WE DIE

I remember exactly where I was when the question popped into my mind seemingly out of nowhere. It wasn't a new question. It is a fairly common question most people ponder at some point. This was a strange question only because I thought I already knew the answer.

The details of the day are vivid. I was on one of my afternoon listening walks in the neighborhood. It was a warm, sunny day. There was an elementary school to my right and cars passing by on my left. I was wearing headphones and listening to an audiobook unrelated to death, dying, or life after death.

The question made such a humble entrance I could have easily mistaken it for just another passing thought. As I would learn, subtlety is a hallmark of how ideas come to me when I listen. They are simple and direct with little fanfare.

Having attended thousands of sermons, Vacation Bible Schools, church camps, and Sunday School classes over my lifetime, I thought I had a pretty good grasp of Christianity's theology of the afterlife. So why was this question coming up now? I wasn't sick and dying. No one

I knew was on death's door. But the question persisted for days to the point of becoming an obsession. I am neither an anxious nor obsessive person, so it feels unnatural when something relentlessly nags at me.

I understand now the answers I was taught as a child about what happens when we die, where we go, and ideas of the afterlife were anemic at best. The choices were either we go to heaven to be with God for eternity or go to hell and be tortured by the Devil forever. There was no discussion whatsoever about what happens once we're over there. Angels, mostly guardian angels, were briefly mentioned but quickly marginalized so as not to trip on the religious rule forbidding the worshiping of angels. The souls of departed loved ones were also another rarely mentioned but dicey category. The idea that grandma could serve as spiritual advisors who could help, love, and support from afar just as they did when they were on Earth was considered blasphemous.

According to those on the other side, many of the views of the afterlife I was taught were not *not* accurate but inadequate. To use an analogy, my overly simplistic beliefs about the afterlife were like saying the ocean has water in it. That is not *not* true, but man, does it miss a whole lot of detail.

I eventually took the question of what happens when we die to my therapist. She found it a perfectly healthy question and suggested I read the book *After* by Bruce Greyson, M.D. about his research into near-death experiences. I thoroughly enjoyed the book, but it didn't provide the clarity I sought. Dr. Greyson's book is an excellent research-based, clinically driven book on near-death experiences. I highly recommend it.

I mentioned to a friend that I was reading Dr. Greyson's book. She, too, had read it and enjoyed it. Then her face lit up and she asked, "But have you read *The Light Between Us* by Laura Lynne Jackson?" I had not nor had I ever heard of the book or the author.

A few days later, I found the book at the local library. From the very first page, I was hooked. Mrs. Jackson is a precious soul. She taught high school English for sixteen years while operating as a clandestine psychic medium on nights and weekends. She kept her abilities secret because she feared personal and professional consequences.

The subject matter of *The Light Between Us* is heavy. Much of her psychic work at the time revolved around connecting parents of deceased children with grieving parents. She worked with a group called *The Forever Family Foundation* which provides free gatherings that bring together certified psychics with grieving parents to connect with their children who have crossed over to the other side. She also submitted her psychic abilities to rigorous testing by the Windbridge Institute, where she and a handful of other psychic mediums were certified as having significant psychic abilities.

The stories in her book were captivating but also devastating. As a father of four, if I were to lose a child I would do anything and move heaven and earth to reconnect with my beautiful child. Nothing equals the pain and devastation of a parent losing a child.

At certain moments while reading her book I felt completely overwhelmed with emotion. I was so moved by the accounts of parents and children reuniting that I found myself crying so hard I was gasping for air. This was not normal crying. Something important was moving in my heart.

I make no bones about the fact that I am a crier. I am not ashamed of it in the least. However, the crying I experienced while reading *The Light Between Us* was beyond normal tearfulness. My emotions were coming from deep within. I felt I had run an emotional marathon by the time I finished the book. But I also felt invigorated in a way I had not felt before. *The Light Between Us* opened the door wide to the clarity I had been seeking about what happens when we die.

During this time, I was going through my divorce, moving into a rental house, and getting my financial life in order. I am certain this played a role in my hypersensitivity at the time. However, life continued on. I had to go to work everyday and do the work to mend my broken heart a little more each day. The holidays were just around the corner and I didn't want to miss a moment with my kids.

Weeks turned into months without pursuing the question of what happens when we die any further. In many ways, I felt I had finally cracked the code. What more did I need to know? While Mrs. Jackson offered tantalizing details about what life is like on the other side, it didn't completely satisfy my curiosity. In fact, it left me wanting more insight and clarity. Mrs. Jackson encouraged her readers that they didn't need a psychic medium to connect with God, spiritual guides, or their departed loved ones. Just talk to them like you would if they were still on Earth, she encouraged. She wrote another book called *Signs* that delved into the topic of how to connect with departed loved ones. For example, if your mother loved turtles when she was alive, use those cute little animals as a sign from your mom when you see one.

After the holidays when life returned to normal, the question also returned with a renewed intensity even greater than before. I started listening to my inner rumblings on the subject which led me to want to know more about the spirit world from the perspective of those who have crossed over.

I am no stranger to the topic of spirituality. It seems this curiosity started for me at a very young age. My mom loves telling a story about me when I was five years old[33]. We were in church and it was nearing the end of the service when the preacher made his altar call. For those unaware of this ritual, this is an impassioned plea by the pastor for anyone to confess their sins and get right with Jesus. My mom says that as the preacher made his pitch, I got up in front of the entire church, made my way to the front, and knelt at the altar. I clasped my little hands together and began praying.

Since starting this adventure in search of answers to the question of what happens when we die, I have had many amazing experiences. I recount some of them in the pages ahead and hope to pass along to you some of the peace I have received to help you navigate this bewildering and beautiful world.

27

THE GOSPEL
ACCORDING TO THE
DEAD

Like many people, my spiritual beliefs have evolved over the decades with life experience and wisdom from the School of Hard Knocks. I was born into an Evangelical Pentecostal charismatic church in rural Arkansas. I grew up in the same type of church when we moved to rural southern Mississippi when I was five years old. In college, I attended a charismatic, nondenominational church. After college, I moved to Nashville, where I attended a Presbyterian church. After many years, I attended a popular nondenominational church on the famous Music Row called Belmont Church. From there, I married and moved to Seattle, Washington, where I attended seminary. This was like being in church every day, eight hours a day. Upon returning to Nashville from Seattle, our family attended an Episcopalian church. After a dozen or so years the priest we dearly loved retired, a schism occurred in the church over gay clergy, the global pandemic crisis happened, and I went through a divorce. Due to these and other circumstances I withdrew my affiliation with organized religion.

Just as the chaos in U.S. politics caused me to give up any affiliation with a political party, I decided I wanted to remain spiritually active and practice Christianity but no longer felt the need to align with a particular denomination. The Us vs. Them lines between denominations and religions conflicted with how I wanted to live. I could no longer align with love, wisdom, and integrity and view people from a different religion or political party as bad, wrong, or the enemy.

Ironically, this movement away from organized religion has invigorated my spiritual life. If asked to describe my spiritual orientation today, the word I feel most comfortable with is mystical. I fully recognize how someone calling themselves a mystic could come across as pompous.

Today, I have more peace and confidence about the good and bad things that come my way. I no longer view difficult experiences as a punishment from a vengeful God or random occurrences in a chaotic universe. Now, I understand that we create a master plan for ourselves before coming to Earth based on what our soul needs to learn. We arranged experiences and relationships to give our souls opportunities to learn. In this way, our pain has a purpose on the most epic scale of eternity.

In some ways, my listening adventure to discover what life is like on the other side has made this life harder to tolerate, not easier. There is a part of my soul that just wants to be done with all of this Earth drama and go home and rest for a very long time. But for now, I am in it to win it! I want to be the best person possible, help and serve as many people as possible, and learn every lesson possible while my soul lives in this incredible body on this beautiful planet.

The Gospel According To The Dead is intended to be an unsettling title. It is a warning flare that we are no longer in the safe harbor of the traditional beliefs. We are venturing into uncharted territory on the outer edges of theology, philosophy, psychology, eschatology, and existentialism.

These are not my ideas. The ideas presented here came from the dead. However, they are only dead from our Earthly perspective. I am grateful for these spiritual pioneers who dare reach through the veil of their world to give us a glimpse of the coming attractions awaiting us all. Their words are full of love and hope yet at times unsettling though not in a terrifying way but an awe-inspiring way.

Many of the ideas the spirits share may challenge traditional beliefs of life, death, and the afterlife. Rather than embracing and exploring their discomfort, some would rather close their hearts and minds out of fear. And you know what? That is okay. When it comes to spiritual matters such as these, very few people will take another person's experience as truth for themselves. I don't expect you to be anywhere other than where you are today. I am opening a door. If you would like to peek inside, go for it. If you want to slam the door shut and run the other way, that's okay too.

Who are these dead souls that supposedly communicate the wonders of the afterlife to us back here on Earth? In the references section at the end of this book, you will find a list of the nearly eighty books I used as research. The subjects vary from dying, death, near-death experiences, the afterlife, eternal souls, psychic mediums, spirit guides, and reincarnation to name just a few topics. There are papers on spirituality written by Albert Einstein and a book by a female civilian employee of the Army Corps of Engineers working alongside soldiers in Iraq who nearly died after the Humvee they were riding in was hit by an improvised explosive device (IED).

But who were these souls while they were on Earth? And who are the people supposedly receiving these messages from the other side? If there is a test of your confidence in these ideas, it will most likely be at this pivotal juncture. You will be required to take a leap of faith and believe that these souls did come back to communicate from beyond the grave and those that hear their voices are honest and truthful.

How do you know this isn't a hoax and these individuals are not simply preying upon everyone's fear of death or grieving families? You can't know the intentions of anyone because in this life, unlike the next, our true intentions are easily hidden from each other. Are there fake psychics out there who prey on the bereaved? Of course. Are there also people who have a genuine ability to connect grieving souls here on Earth with their departed loved ones? I believe so.

Let's return to detailing a few of the sources of information for this book. Psychic medium Laura Lynne Jackson wrote *The Light Between Us* and *Signs.* She was a high school English teacher for sixteen years. The Windbridge Institute certified her after she passed multiple rigorous tests. Much of her work has focused on connecting parents with the souls of their deceased children.

In 1969 Helen Greaves published *Testimony of Light.* She writes about the sudden and unexpected connection with her lifelong friend Sister Frances Banks, who was a nun in South Africa for many decades. Sister Frances Mary, as she was known in the convent, taught psychology courses in colleges and served in prisons. After her passing, she returned to her friend, who was as surprised as anyone by her return. Helen Greaves had not written anything similar before her experience with her friend Sister Frances Mary. One of the most profound and encouraging insights I learned during my research came from Sister Frances Mary. She said, "When you learn a lesson in this life, you learn it for all eternity." This idea brings me great comfort and peace, knowing that all the work we do to overcome and learn from life's most difficult experiences is not in vain.

Dr. Bruce Greyson is a Professor Emeritus of Psychiatry and Neurobehavioral Sciences at the University of Virginia, Carlson Professor Emeritus of Psychiatry & Neurobehavioral Sciences, and Former Director of the Division of Perceptual Studies. His research into near-death experiences led to him writing the book *After.*

Tyler Henry is a young man with exceptional abilities chronicled on the highly successful Netflix series *Life After Death.* He came from humble beginnings in an area that didn't look kindly on people who were different, whether it was their psychic abilities or sexual orientation. His journey into the world of psychic mediumship nearly ended before it began, as he contemplated suicide for years as a teenager due to bullying in school.

Leslie Stringfellow died at twenty in 1906, leaving behind his grieving parents. His father was a world-renowned horticulturist who pioneered fruit and nut cultivation, writing several successful books on the subject. A few years after his death, his parents established contact with him, communicating for more than fifteen years. After a series of bizarre, interrelated events, Stephen J. Chism ended up writing about the Stringfellow's experience in *The Afterlife Of Leslie Stringfellow.*

Dannion Brinkley was, by all descriptions, a terror. He was violent as a youth and became even more violent as a highly trained assassin in the U.S. Army, where he tracked and killed people in covert operations around the world. In one instance, when he could not kill a dignitary of a foreign country, he blew up a hotel, killing fifty people in the process of assassinating his target.

Dannion chronicles his life story and near-death experiences in his books *Saved By The Light* and *At Peace In The Light.* His experience with spirits from the other side after being struck by lightning caused a radical change in his life, where he began to bring healing and comfort to thousands of dying veterans on their deathbed.

When I made listening to myself a priority I signed up for an adventure without knowing the itinerary. Reflecting back on all that has happened I can truthfully say this has been one of the most rewarding experiences of my life right up there with having kids. After my divorce I needed a spiritual reboot. Obviously, what I was doing wasn't working. Every day I listened and listened and listened for the faintest sound, the still small voice of a God I believed was there. It was in those broken moments of defeat that love, wisdom, and integrity rescued me. I am not hostile toward any part of my spiritual heritage but neither do I have a desire to recreate my new spiritual life based on past experiences. The spirituality of my youth, young adult, and adult life was not replaced, only updated in such a way as to give me greater hope and deeper faith.

28

THE AFTERLIFE: DYING & DEATH

When it comes to death and dying, the spirits communicate that how a person dies is sometimes very important, but most of the time it is not. Someone who lived an extraordinary life but died suddenly or traumatically does not want their memory to be defined by how they died. When a family member or friend cannot move past how their loved one died, it saddens the deceased. Spirits understand that during the time just after death, both the living and the dead need time to acclimate to their new realities.

During the initial shock of grief and loss, usually lasting several weeks, it is not optimal for a spirit to attempt contact with the bereaved. Signs are easily missed during this time because the person grieving is overwhelmed by the agony of their suffering.

The spirits explain that grief is so powerful and the pain of loss so shocking that it blocks a person from receiving their messages. The optimal time to connect with a departed loved one is after the intensity of the grief has subsided however long that might be.

Souls who die suddenly or unexpectedly may feel confused when they first crossover. They may linger on Earth to give themselves time to acclimate to this new reality while watching over their loved ones.

Many souls report wanting to watch over their loved ones and comfort them as much as possible. Initially, this is reassuring and makes their transition from this life to the next easier. But after a while, the lingering becomes more frustrating than helpful because of the soul's inability to physically connect with their loved ones or let them know they are there in an obvious, concrete manner. Eventually, these disembodied spirits are encouraged but never forced by advanced spirits to complete their transition and go to the loving light.

The lingering experience of spirits staying around after death is not typical for someone sick and bedridden for an extended period. Those who have had ample time to ponder their death, are in physical pain, and have had time to say their goodbyes are ready to move on. No loitering needed.

Another example where a deceased spirit may choose to linger on Earth is accidental death by drug overdose. These spirits are shocked that they continue to live on and are often fearful of what comes next. Many were taught religious teachings about hell and judgment and would rather remain in limbo than face the possibility of eternal damnation in the afterlife. Their refusal to enter the loving light is due to fear. When people talk about ghosts, this is one type of "ghost" that haunts the Earth because they refuse to crossover.

Sensitive and young souls who had a traumatic life and/or death may be met in the spirit world by animals. We all know the sense of unconditional love we receive from pets. They serve a similar role in the afterlife. Some souls need a more gentle entrance and animals provide that comfort.

The newly deceased are often surprised and disoriented by how familiar the afterlife looks to their life on Earth. This similarity is a temporary state created solely to help souls transition. Due to this, many souls struggle to comprehend that they are actually dead.

Their new body is similar to their earthly body in both look and feel but is also fundamentally different. Their new body has the same shape as their old one but is only a covering like a costume an actor might wear in a play. This, too, is intended to help in a soul's transition. The essence of a soul is pure energy, but evidently being a blob of energy immediately after death is not as comforting as having arms, legs, hands, and a familiar face.

The newly deceased souls need time to relearn how to move around, communicate telepathically, and learn the laws of their new spiritual reality. As a soul progresses into higher realms, the need for a human body lessens as they return to their true essence.

Along with a body, the newly departed souls carry the essence of who they were on Earth. In other words, our personality persists beyond the grave. In addition to our temperament enduring, other aspects of our identity continue as well.

One disturbing aspect of the spiritual life after death is that we continue to carry the issues we struggled with on Earth into the afterlife. This is why facing our problems and doing our work while on Earth is vitally important. Spirits communicate that working on issues like addictions is much easier on Earth than in the afterlife because this life offers an accelerated environment to correct unwanted character flaws. Spirits urge us to live good lives, love others, and learn life's lessons. If we don't, we may need to return to complete our unfinished business.

I found one story about a group of recalcitrant youth refusing to leave Earth humorous. Instead of transitioning to the spirit world, these youth stayed behind, congregating at their high school. The psychic medium who connected with the teenagers questioned why they remained on Earth. They said this is where all the kids hang out and they wanted to be with their friends. When pressed further, they admitted they were worried it would be boring "in heaven".

During this conversation, the medium connected with an adult spirit among the children. When asked who she was and what she was doing there, she replied that she was a teacher in her previous life, and some of these were her students. She felt obligated to watch over them in their lingering state. In death, as in life, we always have free will to make choices.

When someone dies by suicide, mental and/or physical illness is typically involved. The individual typically isn't well and no longer wants to suffer. The problem with suicide is that it interrupts the life plan they agreed to before coming to Earth. Suicide is almost universally frowned upon by spirits on the other side. Certain circumstances of suffering related to pain and terminal illness, for example, may be acceptable but only rarely. However, generally speaking, suicide is checking out of your life plan too early. This seems especially important for children and young adults. What is impossible for these young souls to comprehend amid severe psychological suffering is that they chose this particular path to see if they could overcome the temptation to end their lives and grow from the experience.

The most profound reason not to commit suicide is that it does not solve any problems. Once you are on the other side, you realize all you managed to accomplish by killing yourself was delaying opportunities for your spiritual growth that you must eventually confront and correct. Problems have a way of following you throughout eternity until you work through them. The old proverb of being unable to outrun your problems seems true in heaven as on Earth.

Souls who checked out of life early feel tremendous sadness at having left an opportunity to correct flaws and advance. If you ever find yourself negotiating with someone who is suicidal, tell them it won't solve any of their problems. It will only postpone them until they are ready to do the work necessary to heal. Do not worry about offending them. Think of the alternative if they follow through with their plan.

Our purpose on Earth is to transform our spiritual consciousness from a less evolved level to a more evolved level. This isn't about hierarchy or competition as we have on Earth. The only person you are competing against is yourself.

After we die, souls are encouraged to take time to recover and regenerate their spirit's energy. One of the first emotions spirits report feeling after they die is a great sense of relief. They compare the Earth experience to a long, hard trip and returning home to a hot shower, home-cooked meal, and your own bed.

Spirits say there are many other places besides Earth throughout the universe where spirits can go to be tested. Some of these worlds are psychologically demanding, while others are physically challenging. Spirits say that Earth is both psychologically *and* physically challenging, making it a very difficult training ground for the soul.

One final thought on death. No one dies alone. The spirits say that whatever religious or spiritual belief you choose on Earth will manifest in some form upon your death. Christians can expect to be met by other Christians and many Christian symbols. The same is true for Muslims, Hindus, and Buddhists. This is not a hard and fast rule of what every soul will experience but holds true for most.

A few final thoughts on the soul's passage into death. As mentioned, some souls refuse to go to the light for various reasons. There is a category of people who flatly refuse to acknowledge they are dead because their beliefs about death don't line up with what they are experiencing. These discarnate souls stay on Earth and are another category of souls that become what we call ghosts. These spirits are trapped and, more often than not, unhappily wandering Earth alone, refusing any encouragement to continue on their journey to the loving light.

The spirits also warn about deathbed confessions. They are adamant that deathbed confessions do not work. A few final words from a fear-filled soul who knows they are about to die does not indicate a life lived in pursuit of love, wisdom, and integrity. Be aware that simply saying a few words in prayer will not erase how you lived. You will be required to answer for your life.

Even though a vast chasm separates the living and the dead, there is a simple way for anyone to connect with their departed loved ones. You can pray for them. There are many reasons why souls need us to pray for them. One is that souls are pure energy and prayer is a form of energy. When we pray for those we love, we give them fuel for their journey. It brings those souls great joy to be remembered by their loved ones. Love truly is above all and is eternal.

Remember, your departed loved ones are nearby when you need them, even if you don't feel them. You can call on them for help or answers or peace or guidance. Just ask. They are eager to help you because they love you. By helping you, they are also helping themselves along on their journey.

Your prayers matter. Remember that. Pray for yourself. Pray for your loved ones. Pray for the deceased. Pray for peace and love. Pray for me and I'll pray for you!

29

THE AFTERLIFE: LIFE REVIEW

A soul's preparation for coming to Earth is extensive. While time in the afterlife and Earth differ, those dimensions overlap when a soul takes on human form. It takes planning for the many variables to align just right for a soul to enter the body at the optimal time for their greatest benefit.

The soul has many choices to consider when planning an Earth life. They get to choose which city they will be born, their specific talents, their physical appearance, temperament, profession, life partners, friends and family, and adversaries and enemies that will teach them lessons. There is also the consideration of the placement of planets and stars and how the planetary alignment will impact events in a person's life. A soul can choose some of the adversities they will experience and multiple exit points for their death. These are just a few considerations a soul must make when coming to this world. Each decision is carefully considered for the perfection of the soul.

When a body dies and the soul returns to the spirit world, they are greeted by loved ones. They also need time to rest, repair, and rejuvenate their energy. Sooner or later, souls are compelled to complete a *Life Review* after their return from Earth.

Life Reviews happen in different places. Some occur in solitary, quiet environments similar to Earth's libraries. Other times, souls have *Life Reviews* at the moment of their death, reliving each experience scene-by-scene.

In the library-like settings, there are books similar to what we have on Earth. However, these books are more interactive, showing events from a person's life in an animated, movie-like form that can be stopped, reversed, and fast-forwarded.

One aspect of *Life Reviews* that are consistent no matter when or how they occur is that you not only review your life but feel each experience from the different perspectives of those involved. For example, if you committed a crime and harmed someone, you would live out that event from your perspective as the perpetrator but also the perspective of the victim. This is true for positive, uplifting moments as well as selfish, cruel acts. This is why it is vitally important to treat everyone with loving-kindness while on Earth. Everything you did will be revealed and relived in full in the next life during your *Life Review*.

It is helpful to think of your life plan in terms of architectural blueprints. You have one set of blueprints you created for yourself before coming to Earth. You have another set of blueprints for how your life turned out. When you die and conduct your *Life Review,* these two blueprints are transposed on top of one another to see how your actual life compared to your planned life. The spirits talk about how shocking and unsettling this experience can be for a soul once they realize all of the missed opportunities and dead-end roads taken.

In hindsight, the path you planned for yourself will seem so obvious. It is humbling to see how far off the preplanned path you wandered at times, all the while believing you were on the right path. These realizations, while disappointing, become the motivation for future incarnations and spiritual work necessary to advance your soul.

30

THE AFTERLIFE - JUDGMENT, HELL, JUSTICE & MERCY

There is likely no subject that conjures up more fear in so many as the idea of an eternal hell. We have all stuck our fingers in an exposed light socket or burned ourselves on a hot stove. Those few brief seconds were horrible. The idea of such torture going on forever is dreadful. It is understandable why many people choose to play it safe and just tow the party line regarding religion.

I rejected hell in principle when I was young. I could not integrate the idea of a loving God torturing me forever if I did something as insignificant as saying a curse word. The punishment didn't fit the crime.

As I grew older, my protests against the idea showed itself through a lackluster interest in religion. At times, my resolve weakened and I operated hypocritically. Due to my own fears about hell, I stayed close enough to the pews to jump right in a seat if necessary. I was not immune to the instinctual fear of eternal torture. Through my studies into the afterlife, I found a hell I could believe in and wholeheartedly support.

When the spirits talk about God, they become animated. They want to convey that there is a force that is the source of all things, but they do not like the name God. They talk about how, on Earth, this term has become too personalized to a physical being. They speak of God not as a deity but as the essence of everything and in all things. They prefer to call God *The Source Of All Things* or simply *The Source.*

In the spirit's attempt to describe God in terms we can understand, they use what we are familiar with to describe the unfamiliar. They speak of God as an all-loving presence but expand that idea by describing *The Source* as even greater than love!

There are realms of realities in the afterlife. The beings in the higher realms have become more perfect, more like *The Source,* through their spiritual work. Beings in these higher realms can communicate to beings in lower realms, but it is not common. Everyone is busy doing their work.

The spirits speak of an awareness that something greater exists, but many cannot see it, nor do they want to. They sense drawing close to it would be too intense for their present state to handle and so have a healthy respect for the immensity and power of *The Source.* They are content to be in their realm, learning and enjoying the beauty, rest, play, and work without all the heaviness of Earth life.

The spirits report that you cannot hide your true self once on the other side. Your true essence is on display for all to see. That is why spirits go to specific areas where souls are generally similar. This is also why justice *and* mercy are vital.

On Earth, as we pass our tests, we achieve a new level of spiritual wisdom that allows us to elevate our souls toward greater perfection. The same principle applies in the afterlife as well. We can work to advance our souls and elevate them to the higher realms of the spirit world. But what about those who have committed horrible acts, causing others, possibly many, to suffer and have no remorse?

There is a high priority placed on the free will of a soul. The ability for souls to choose as they desire creates more chaos but also more love in this world. There are two possible explanations for pain and suffering in the world. The first explanation is that we chose an experience for ourselves because we wanted to face a test, learn something from the experience, or be part of another soul's learning experience. The second path is that souls whose energy is damaged in some way may use their free will for evil. This path creates chaos and is not part of any soul's original plan. Conundrums such as these are what makes life on Earth so challenging to comprehend.

The idea of a corrupted soul is not hard for us to imagine. We don't need to guess. Search the headlines of any news website and you will be accosted by unbelievable acts of evil. What then happens to a soul that is so lost it is irredeemable?

Many aspects of the afterlife are not known even to the spirits. In these cases, we must make sweeping generalizations based on small clues. Corrupt souls are one of those instances where we must extrapolate a lot based on a little. A soul that is corrupt must be dealt with differently than most other souls. The energy of a corrupt soul is repurposed in some way through a process where it is not destroyed, but neither is it what it used to be. It seems this is both justice and mercy in action.

The spirits report about different areas of the spirit realm. One spirit playfully calls the place souls go immediately after death *Summerland* because it is always sunny. I admit it does sound like a theme park in Florida. However, the place Christians call hell the spirits call *Shadowland.*

How a person lives their life determines whether or not they end up in the *Shadowlands.* But even this isn't as binary as we were taught in Sunday School. Good people do bad things all the time. You have probably done something you are ashamed of and could be considered by some as evil. That doesn't make you an evil person. How you respond to your negative experiences makes all the difference. Do you seek forgiveness and redemption or continue your destructive behaviors?

People who commit one evil act after another without remorse lack the humility to own their mistakes, make amends, and learn from the experience. This is what gets people exiled to *Shadowland*. It would be overly simplistic to call these people evil and that place hell. They are, after all, a creation of *God, The Source Of All Things.*

Shadowland is a place set apart from *Summerland.* The spirits report that the souls in *Shadowland* suffer, but it is not a suffering of their own making. This is a critically important point and what makes it so different from the hell many are taught in Sunday School.

One of *Shadowland's* most profound and confounding aspects is that souls can leave this dreadful place any time they choose. The requirements for leaving are to accept responsibility for their actions and do the arduous work necessary to make amends and be more loving. However, like drug addicts on Earth, many souls choose the misery of their self-made hell rather than the peace and healing found in the work of sobriety.

The physicality of *Shadowland* is dreadfully bleak. It is filled with fear and a place where souls harm other souls. One story the spirits reported was of a man who murdered a young woman. The mother of the deceased woman chose to live above him in *Shadowland.* Every day, she would come down to where he lived and beat him for what he did to her daughter. The sad irony was that both souls were trapped in a hell of their own making, the man by his evil, murderous act and the mother by her unwillingness to forgive her daughter's perpetrator.

Most souls steer clear of *Shadowland.* However, some charitable souls venture into this hellish place of suffering to attempt to retrieve lost souls. They share how their suffering can end at any moment of their choosing if they would only follow them into the loving light. These missionary souls only go to these places with protector angels because it seems that without them, it would be too dangerous.

Why souls choose to stay in these horrible places is beyond me, but the fact that there is such a place both comforts and disturbs me. I don't want a hell-like place to exist, but I understand it needs to exist. Light needs darkness. Goodness needs evil. Heaven needs hell.

Shadowland is stunning to me for several reasons. First, it is astonishing that a place such as this even exists. I had written hell off as a way to scare people into giving their allegiance and money to a church. This version of hell seems both just and merciful. Second, no one puts anyone in *Shadowland.* It is a place we put ourselves by our actions. The beauty of this is that you can also get yourself out. Theologian C. S. Lewis knew something of this when he wrote, "The gates of hell are locked from the inside." Third, another surprising fact is that some people venture into these dark places to retrieve lost souls. The spirits say this selfless act of retrieving lost souls will continue until every soul has been reclaimed from the *Shadowlands.* Wow! What a beautiful act of love!

31

THE AFTERLIFE - WHEN CHILDREN DIE

A strong word of caution before you proceed. If you have lost a child or are close to someone who recently lost a child, I suggest you skip this chapter for now. This information could trigger a traumatic episode if you are in the grip of the monster that is grief.

The spirits have a lot to say about the death of children. Their words are profound and healing. They can comfort those who have lost a child if heard at the right time. As affirming as their words are, they do not take away the cataclysmic suffering grieving parents endure because of the absence of their little earth angel.

Time after time, the spirits implore that most souls cross over when it is their chosen time. They double down on this when it is a tragic and traumatic passing, especially of a child.

The spirits talk about an understanding for the young soul once they have transitioned to the afterlife. They understand their life and death in the context of the plan for their soul and the souls of others. This does not mean that all souls who died young planned to leave early. The free will mentioned earlier is a very difficult concept to comprehend when it comes to the loss of life, especially for someone so young.

Psychic Medium George Anderson tells the story of a session he conducted with an Army veteran of the war in Afghanistan. During one deployment, this soldier found himself at an elementary school full of young children passing out candy. As he posed next to a young Afghan girl, his platoon was ambushed. The girl he was standing next to was struck by a barrage of bullets and died instantly.

In his session with Mr. Anderson, the girl came through for the soldier, telling him she was now one of his spirit guides on the other side. She encouraged him to stop feeling sorry for her and heal his heart so he might overcome his addictions. She said that the drugs and alcohol he was abusing to cope with his guilt would never be enough. He must accept that what happened had a purpose and let go of his guilt and shame.

This little girl shared with the soldier that he played a part in actually saving her life. The soldier was confused because his presence caused this little girl and many other children to die that day.

The girl shared with him that she did not have a good life on Earth. She had none of the opportunities American girls had and it was a grace for her to leave this world so young. She relayed how the place she was in now was full of life and opportunities. She is safe and happy with other children. She is glad she is no longer on Earth.

Psychic Medium Rebecca Rosen offered this insight in her newsletter soon after the Uvalde school shooting, "In my years as a spiritual medium I have heard Spirit relay the message that our greatest challenges and heartbreaks, even something as horrible as murder, are full of meaning and purpose, and can result in our spiritual growth, learning, and blessings."

As long as we are on Earth in human form, we will never see the grand plan at work and the purpose and meaning behind seemingly incomprehensible tragedies. As a result, we must grope around in the dark, trying to make sense of life where we can and accept that there are things we cannot know. This is deeply unsatisfying in the face of tragedy, yet this, too, is part of the spiritual maturation process. To not know why something happened and still trust there is an intelligent design to all that happens is an epic leap of trust in *The Source Of All Things.*

One final thought on children in the afterlife. When children pass over, they are met by wise and compassionate souls who are their guides and teachers. There are schools for children similar to schools on Earth where children can be with other children. In these schools, they learn and laugh and play. As mentioned, children are often greeted by animals first when they cross over due to their unconditional love.

32

THE AFTERLIFE - LIFE AFTER LIFE

Our life after our brief stint here in Earth school is our real life. Everything that happens to us here on Earth makes sense in the afterlife. We gain a fuller understanding of and appreciation for our true nature as eternal beings.

Spirits say that time in the afterlife differs significantly from time on Earth. Here, time is linear, but in the afterlife, time happens all at once unless you want to change the quality of time and experience it linearly. If that is true, all you need to do is change your consciousness and time switches from everything all at once to linear.

According to spirits, the afterlife has schools similar to Earth's universities. There are grand assemblies dedicated to the arts and others to the sciences. Souls who were great in these endeavors on Earth put on performances and teach classes. Mozart could be giving a concert while Matisse teaches an art class. There are team sports to play. The games are similar to Earth games but played with energy instead of physical objects. The emphasis is on the team and not the individual.

There are libraries and grand halls for singing and worship. There are places for receiving souls and places for healing souls. There are mountains, grass, trees, birds, and fields where wild animals roam.

Music is the language everyone understands. Music isn't simply an auditory experience but a felt energy that vibrates and communicates meaning. Everyone can sing and be a part of the great harmonizing of souls.

There is romantic love in the afterlife. There are stories about lovers and spouses eagerly awaiting their partner's return. There is reportedly even new love to be found as well.

There are libraries full of books, but books that act as three-dimensional archives that can be stopped, fast-forwarded, and re-wound. There are rooms with giant video-like screens that can give potential future outcomes of possible lives when someone is debating whether or not to come, or return, to Earth. Reincarnation on Earth is a choice and only recommended if it is the best path for a soul to learn. Not every soul needs to return.

Will you reincarnate? It depends.

33

THE AFTERLIFE - REINCARNATION

Reincarnation is another one of the no-no categories for Evangelical Christians. The rejection of this belief is based on the actions of the Second Ecumenical Council of Constantinople in 553 A.D. The Catholic church denies that reincarnation was addressed during this meeting, stating that the official record does not mention the subject. However, anyone who has ever been bullied can attest the psychological stress of the threat of the bully can spread fear, which is equal to the harm of physical violence.

It is true the theology of reincarnation was not officially banned at this council. Instead, there were behind-the-scenes political maneuvers by the council to silence anyone who dared to continue teaching reincarnation:

It is believed that in 553 A.D. during the
Second Council of Constantinople, the idea
of reincarnation was found to have no place
in the Christian Church. Although reincar-
nation was not officially rejected at this
council, those early Church Fathers who
were accused of teaching the idea of reincar-
nation had their works banned. 553 A.D. did
mark the end of the debate on reincarnation
within the Christian community.

It appears the council resorted to theological thuggery to get their way. Through book banning and misuse of power to obfuscate outcomes, they created a hostile environment that manipulated the result to their liking. We may not have advanced all that much in 1500 years.

Christians believe death is a one-way door through which no one can return. Historically, this goes against the teachings of early Christians and other major spiritual belief systems, such as Egyptians. But even more convincing to our modern sensibilities are the decades of thorough, validated research from people like Jim Tucker, M.D.

Dr. Tucker is a child psychiatrist and Bonner-Lowry Professor of Psychiatry and Neurobehavioral Sciences at the University of Virginia School of Medicine. His research into reincarnation offers solid scientific evidence that even the most hardened skeptic would have difficulty refuting. For more detailed information, I suggest his book *Before*.

Dr. Tucker writes research-based books, not fiction thrillers. His sometimes dry prose takes a certain determination to get through much like a good bowl of steel cut oatmeal. But that is what is needed for such a controversial subject as past lives and reincarnation. Even though we live in a post-truth world, data on topics such as reincarnation are essential to include in conversations on matters related to spirituality.

Dr. Tucker and his team have cataloged many cases of children who have memories of past lives, the details of which they could not have realistically known. Of all the possible explanations, reincarnation is the most logical option.

Here again, Christians fail to offer sufficient answers to valid questions about the journey of a soul. Christians universally believe we have a soul, and that soul is eternal. But what is that eternal soul supposed to do with all its time?

From a practical perspective, reincarnation seems necessary. One life is not nearly long enough for a soul to become spiritually mature. How many people do you know who get to the end of their lives and don't seem to have learned much about loving themselves and others? It is easy to see the value of living multiple lives under different circumstances. This unique perspective gives invaluable insight and compassion for the suffering of others. In one life, you might be a wealthy white man. In another life, you might come as a disabled black child in the South. These would give you radically different experiences from which to learn.

The spirits tell us that reincarnation can serve as a method of justice. Those who have committed terrible acts of violence in one life may need to come back to make amends for their actions by reincarnating in a life similar to that of their victim so they may experience the pain they inflicted. This is yet another complicated concept to comprehend. Only a being with more knowledge than a human could make sense of such a paradox.

When looking at all the data on reincarnation, anyone with an objective point of view would conclude that it seems reasonable, possible, and probable.

34

CASE STUDY #2: PLANT MEDICINE

On August 12, 2022, I died.

Before the final moment of death, I found myself far more afraid than I expected. Out of fear, I raised my hand to signal to my friend who was sitting with me that I needed him to come over. I needed his comforting presence. I needed to be held like a frightened child.

My friend came over and sat next to me. I clutched his hands and curled into a fetal position like a wild animal that had dragged itself into the woods, knowing its end was near. All I could do was close my eyes and wait.

We sat together as I drifted in and out of consciousness. The room was quiet and the quiet was peaceful. At some point, I felt his grip loosen every so slightly. The movement startled me and I pleaded with him through blurry, tear-filled eyes, "Just a little bit longer?" He smiled, nodded, and once again held my hand.

The next time I felt him letting go, I didn't resist. I knew he had walked with me as far as he could go. I was grateful I hadn't been alone, but I knew I had to go the rest of the way alone.

Words fail to capture what happened next. How do you explain nothingness and nonexistence? I only know that I ceased to exist. If you have ever experienced anesthesia, think of those few moments before losing consciousness, then nothing. I was in the nothingness.

At some point, I realized I was moving toward a vast, dark nothingness. I could feel a vacuum-filled void drawing closer. My thoughts were fading. My ego was vanishing. My identity of who I had been all my life was slipping away. I was going, going, and then I was gone. In this inky void, time had no meaning, nor did I take up any physical space. I had no memory of the past, no recognition of the present, or concept of the future. It was as if I never existed.

The only way I became aware I was in this void was because of the undefined organic shapes around me that I knew were there but could not identify. Everything was a dense dark gray on dark brown on dark black. I could barely discern a single detail. I did notice movement among the shapes.

The awareness that I was moving in a direction going somewhere began to emerge. I recognized the ambiguous forms were cloud-like. The sensation I felt was of flying through clouds at night. It may be more accurate to say I was being pulled through them as I had no will to do anything except experience what was happening.

The clouds slowly became more distinct and I realized I was passing through a transitional gateway. I came to realize that it was me who was flying through this space. I also had an awareness that I was no longer on Earth. I don't know where I traveled through, but I was me again. I was Reb. I was the person I had always been, but somehow different.

As I emerged from this gray gateway, I found myself floating in the vastness of space. I was in what felt like nighttime on Earth. It was dark but not pitch black. There were tiny flickers of light all around. The darkness was silent and peaceful.

As I floated in space, I began to have a strange awareness. My body looked human, but I knew it was only a container for my soul. My body slowly tilted backward as if I were lying down. My gaze turned upward and I began to gently float upwards. The first thing I noticed were the lights. There were millions and millions of lights everywhere like little stars, far too many to count.

As I continued my slow upward ascent, I felt the extraordinary sensations of love and awe. It was a strange combination of reverential fear and wonder. Part of the fear was the overwhelming sensation of joy and pleasure. It was beyond anything I had ever experienced and almost more than my body could hold. My back arched while I made involuntary moaning and groaning noises as my body continued to rise higher and higher.

I was not in control of anything that was happening. I had not been in control of anything since leaving Earth, yet I was not afraid but in awe. Everything was happening in slow motion, including my thoughts. I began to have a dawning awareness of my body rising higher. As I floated upward, my gaze became fixed on the lights above. It was communicated to me telepathically that the lights were not stars as I had assumed. Each light was an eternal soul.

I looked left and then right. I looked up and then down. I noticed how the sky bent downward slightly at its farthest edges. I was under the impression that I was in some gigantic celestial dome. Words cannot capture the size and sensation of being in this magnificent holy place. Later, as I grasped for some way to describe this place, I came to call it the *Hall of All Souls*.

Then a dawning realization occurred to me, I had completed my journey. I had transformed from earthling through death's dark portal and transitioned into the afterlife. I was on the other side. I finally knew from experience the answer to the question that had become my obsession on Earth, "What happens when we die?"

I remained in the *Hall Of All Souls* for quite some time. I remember sounds like music and voices combined, maybe the same thing. It was a penetrating sound that carried an emotion unlike any sound I ever heard on Earth. It was alive. It was life itself.

I do not remember how long I remained in the *Hall of All Souls*, but I eventually transitioned to a pure white space. It is difficult to call this place a room because it had no walls, floor, or ceiling, but it felt like I was inside some kind of structure. This infinitely white space was beautiful and peaceful. It was in this space that I met my father. There was an instant recognition between us. We embraced each other with the intensity of two long-lost souls reunited. As we held each other, I felt an overwhelming rush of love for my father. In life, we had missed each other so many times. He was a principled, dutiful father, always providing financially but emotionally guarded and, at times, rigid and harsh. I was emotional and prone to dreaming like my mother. As father and son, we were often at odds and never really connected in this life.

In this loving moment, my father and I embraced. As we held each other, I sensed a voice from somewhere strong and firm come to me with a message. The voice said, "It is time to love your father unconditionally." As my father held me, I relaxed in his arms and let him hold me without reservation. I allowed my father to be my dad and made the choice to love him unconditionally.

From this white room, I transitioned into what can only be described as a rugby scrum. I was huddled in a tightly packed mass of souls numbering twelve. We were all rocking from side to side in unison. Everyone was laughing as if we had just won a big game. The mood was upbeat and rowdy, like a party.

Standing across from me was my friend who had walked me up to death's door. He was the energetic leader of this group. He smiled at me with a knowing grin. We didn't talk, but he communicated with me telepathically that this whole experience had been a setup in the best possible way. I didn't know if he was talking about my death, this afterlife experience, or my entire life on Earth!

I flashed on a memory of a previous conversation with this friend. In that conversation that occurred on Earth, I was shown how I often lead with my ego and intellect and how this can separate me from genuinely connecting with others. This heady ego-driven energy of mine prevents me from seeing life through other people's eyes. Back in the scrum, my friend communicated to me telepathically how these ego-driven experiences are setups for lessons I needed to learn and he was part of setting them up! The scrum was a fun place and I wanted to stay there but soon after that realization I was taken to a dark place.

The place I was taken to felt like it was somewhere on Earth many years before my current life. I found myself looking down through a sewer grate or water drain. There was something below in the darkness moving around. As I drew closer, I saw it was a small child, a boy, playing with sticks or a toy.

The setting was dark like night with precious little light. I seemed to be in a city in the Middle East hundreds of years before my current life on Earth. The same voice that told me it was time to love my father unconditionally came to me again. The voice told me this little boy playing in the gutter underneath the street was me in a past life. I was sold into slavery as a child for the pleasure of other people. The voice gently let me know that it was necessary for my current life that I know this information.

As this voice shared this information with me, a group of spirit beings formed a line between me and the boy with their backs to me. They were all wearing brown tunics with their hoods up. I couldn't see their faces. They communicated to me, again telepathically, that what they were doing was for my protection. I was not allowed to see anything that happened to the child. I felt tremendous sorrow for that little boy.

I was taken from this place and led to a scene where I had a realization about my mother. It was communicated to me that my mother made a great sacrifice by coming to Earth. My mother agreed as part of her soul's journey to come to Earth and connect my father and me. She was to be the loving bond that held us together. One of her primary jobs in this lifetime was to bring my father and me together because we both struggle with similar emotional problems of living guarded, isolative lives. My mother was sent as a guide to show us what it means to love and serve others with an open heart. She is the reflection of

Jesus' unconditional love for us on this Earth. This last scene concluded my journey into another realm . . . or so I thought.

As my near-death experience receded, I woke up in a room full of men. We had been on a journey together for the past seven hours, which felt like fifteen minutes. My body was exhausted yet full of life. The sun coming through the windows filled the room with a glorious light.

As I lay awake my eyes drifted around the room taking in the scene. After a few moments I laid back down and stared at the ceiling, I felt awareness returning to my body. I was conscious again. I was myself back on Earth. As I lay there reflecting on all I had witnessed, I was filled with gratitude, wonder, and awe. What had just happened? Was any of it real? Was it all real? It all felt more real than real. But as I was about to learn, my experience was not quite over. Something miraculous was about to happen.

As I lay on my back staring at the ceiling, I saw a spirit hovering over me about twenty feet away. This spirit was floating close to the ceiling and appeared feminine. She was small and made of what appeared to me like translucent, liquid-flowing, clear glass. Her form stayed in constant motion as she floated above me. I could only see her head and torso. She had no arms or legs I could see. While she had a face, it had no expression. She wasn't gazing at me lovingly or expressing any other emotion I could detect. It was comforting to be in her presence. I loved looking at her as I had never seen anything like her before or since. I was amazed, honored, and humbled to be in her presence. Her visitation was one last gift from *The Source*.

In 2000, Johns Hopkins was granted the first regulatory approval to study psychedelics. In 2006, researchers published, *"Psilocybin can occasion mystical-type experiences having substantial and sustained personal meaning and spiritual significance.*" This is considered the landmark study that launched the resurgence of psychedelic research worldwide.

Research on psilocybin shows it is an effective treatment for smoking cessation, major depression, reduction of end-of-life anxiety in those with cancer, and alcohol abuse, to name just a few.

Psilocybin, MDMA, and LSD are in the midst of a revival worldwide due to their general availability, lack of addictive qualities, and at least for psilocybin, have no harmful side effects.

Psilocybin or "Magic Mushrooms" currently exist in a legal gray area in the United States. Cities in Washington state, California, Colorado, Washington D.C., and Massachusetts have passed laws decriminalizing these substances. Decriminalization doesn't make these substances legal. It only prevents authorities from spending money to prosecute individuals for their use or possession.

Psychedelics are powerful medicine. They overwhelm the brain by dissolving the ego. This is what is meant by the phrase ego death. Most people live each day directed by their ego. When someone cuts them off in traffic, for example, and they fly into a rage, that's the ego responding. When someone bumps into you at a bar and it nearly leads to a brawl, that's your ego asserting itself. Your ego is everywhere and can make a mess of things if left unchecked.

The ego is a necessary evil. We need it to operate in our culture because everybody else uses their ego. We would be at a disadvantage if we only acted altruistically. However, there are better tools for the job than the ego. Imagine using a shovel as a hammer. You could do it, but the right tool would do the job better and faster.

In his book *Destiny of Souls,* Michael Newton writes, "We were created and sent to Earth to problem solve within the matrix of an intelligent life form living in a difficult environment which involves suffering but also great beauty and promise. It is this balance we must recognize in our day-to-day reality."

This is a hard life. The spirits acknowledge as much when they cross over to the other side, reporting what a relief it is to be out of this harsh, heavy life on Earth.

In his book *Saved By The Light,* Dannion Brinkley writes of a message given to him by an angel during his near-death experience after being struck by lightning:

> *You humans are truly the heroes. Those who go to Earth are heroes and heroines because you are doing something that no other spiritual beings have the courage to do. You have gone to Earth to co-create with God. We here see everyone who goes to Earth as great adventurers. You had the courage to go and expand your life and take your place in the great adventure that God created known as the world.*

If we could only remember who we were before we were here, our lives would be so different. Instead, we struggle with spiritual amnesia, forgetting our true essence. We cut ourselves off from so much joy and pleasure because we are told it is sinful. We cut ourselves off from each other because we are afraid of getting hurt again. We cut ourselves off from naturally occurring healing substances like psilocybin because the government deemed them harmful sixty years ago.

At that time, the government felt it was necessary to take decisive action on what it considered an existential threat. The country was seeing a surge in drug use and the only way to slow down the firestorm was through legislation. It worked. But is that still necessary about today? The tide is finally turning.

Now, we have respected governments and institutions worldwide researching the power of psychedelics to heal without the strangling grip of pharmaceutical companies scrambling to make as much profit as possible. In many ways, psychedelics present one of the purest paths to healing and spiritual awakening because psilocybin cannot be exploited for profit by corporations.

Finally, can you be a Christian and take a drug like psilocybin?

For older generations, this may be a bridge too far. They grew up in a time of great fear when governments spread salacious falsehoods about how psychedelics would melt their children's brains and cause them to end up in a vegetative state. This sentiment was echoed by religious leaders of the time.

This was a time in our nation when the government and religious institutions were implicitly trusted. This potent cocktail of misinformation mixed with partial truths led this generation to cement a negative view of drugs such as psilocybin.

Today is a different time. Christians should be at the forefront of this healing revolution, not hiding behind outdated beliefs and living in fear. The question remains: Can you be a Christian and take psychedelics? If done in a safe place with trained professionals, I believe this could start a new revival where churches become safe havens for healing from trauma.

Imagine a church-sponsored retreat where individuals are provided spiritual guidance from pastors, ministers, and priests before, during, and after their psychedelic experience. If this were to happen, I believe church pews would be overflowing. The buildings wouldn't be able to hold the masses who would line up to experience a rich and fulfilling spiritual life.

35

LOVE. WISDOM. INTEGRITY.

You were destined to be in this moment right now, reading this book. How do I know? You arranged it before you came to Earth. You placed yourself in this moment because you needed to hear the message that your fate is in your hands.

You came to Earth for a purpose. Your soul had a reason for making the journey when you did, in the particular body you have, in the location you chose, in the family you have, and with many of the experiences you have had and will have. You came here by choice to complete a mission. You set up your life with great intention and thoughtfulness. Your life is not an accident. You put yourself here to do soul work.

When things get hard, remember to ask yourself, "Did I put myself here? If so, why?" then listen and see what you hear. When things are going great, continue asking yourself, "Why did I put myself *here?*" then listen. As Rumi instructs us in his poem *The Guest House*, "Be grateful for whoever comes, because each has been sent as a guide from beyond."

The most painful part of being human is the forgetting. When you crossed the bridge from the energetic immaterial, spiritual world to this physical world of matter, part of the agreement was to relinquish your history as a soul in another dimension. This is necessary to ensure you learn all you need in the shortest time possible but not a second longer. In other words, if you knew everything would work out in the end, you would just run out the clock. It's like getting sued for $100,000 and losing only to have $50,000,000 in the bank. It might sting, but not much. Your life wouldn't change in the least.

But here you are on Earth, often alone, unsure of the future, even less sure about what happens when you die. Whether you accept this truth or not, your destiny is in your hands. We are all blind because we cannot see one second into the future, yet we are required to make decisions in this present moment that will have enormous ramifications for our future. The game is rigged.

You have a life you planned for yourself before coming to Earth and you have the actual life you are living out right now. The life you intended is filled with many beautiful moments, hardships, and heartache. You planned experiences to test yourself. There is free will, which complicates our understanding of pain and suffering, but even if those traumatic experiences were not part of your original plan, they can be transformed into something meaningful by how you go through the experience.

You have the freedom to live your life any way you want. That is what life on Earth is about. However, as soon as you realize you chose to be here and chose this life, the energy of the entire game of life begins to shift in your favor. You see your experiences differently. You see other people in a new light. You gain control of your destiny in a way like never before. The game is still rigged, but now it is rigged in your favor. Once you realize you can't lose, you are playing a whole different game. You transform from victim to victor. Now, you are in control of the only thing you have control over, which is how you respond to a situation and your decisions. This is your superpower.

When making decisions, how do you know which is a good choice and which is a bad choice? Sometimes, it is clear that what you are about to do is wrong. But many times, you will lack such clarity. You have no way of knowing how a particular decision will turn out. There are too many variables outside your control, even for small decisions. This brings us back to the thorn in everyone's side of not being able to know the future.

What, then, are you to do? Dedicate yourself to living your life by the virtues of love, wisdom, and integrity. When you do this, you make choices in the best way possible. You can let your destiny unfold without gripping so tightly to the outcome with fear and anxiety. You have given your *Max Effort* and done all you can do. You will know if you are living by the virtues of love, wisdom, and integrity if you feel a deep and abiding sense of inner peace.

Now, it is time to design your life. It is time for you to take the power of the present moment and craft a destiny to your liking. What does your heart desire? What brings light to your eyes? What do you want to do with your time each day? Your work is to do the work to create a plan to see your destiny manifest.

How do you handle hardships? Feel the raw power of grief, disappointment, and betrayal. Feel it all and feel it deep. That is part of the experience of being human. Feel it now. Let it shape your soul in ways that can only happen in an Earth life. Take heart, sadness and sorrow do not exist in the life after this life.

Let others help you carry your burdens. Let them know you're hurting and feel weak. Let them hold you. When you are once again strong enough to stand on your own, return to doing your daily *Sacred Space* work. Let the sacred source of energy and inspiration found in love, wisdom, and integrity carry you forward into healing and hope. This will work because these virtues contain the power of the living light within us all.

For now, you are back to this day and in this moment on planet Earth. You have work to do. Design your life the way you want it. Seek to align yourself with the life you planned before you arrived here. Grab a pen and journal and get to work. Design your life to the best of your ability, guided by the three virtues. Don't let the gift of your earthly life slip away. Keep doing the work because the work never ends.

You cannot get this life wrong if you live each moment with love, wisdom, and integrity. All of your choices will land somewhere between better and best. Only when you stray from these eternal truths will bad decisions happen, allowing chaos to enter your heart, mind, and life.

Now you know the secret! You are no longer wandering around this life in the dark. The infinite loving *Source* desires for you to climb your *Sacred Mountains.*

Now, it's time for you to listen. Listen to your life. Listen to your body. Listen to your heart. Listen to your friends and family. Listen to the sky and the stars. Listen to the whisper of your departed loved ones. Listen to your pain. Listen to your body. Listen to the silence. Listen to the noise. Listen as your destiny unfolds in the decisions you make every day.

Listen. Listen. Listen.

It is in listening to yourself that you will come to love yourself.

———————— ———————— ————————

May you be loving
May you seek wisdom
May you act with integrity
May you have a courageous heart

REFERENCES

1. *The Light Between Us* - Jackson, Laura Lynne
2. *Signs* - Laura Lynne Jackson
3. *The Artist's Way* - Julia Cameron
4. *People Of The Lie* - M. Scott Peck
5. *Wheels of a Soul* - Rav Berg
6. *After* - Bruce Greyson, M.D.
7. *Before* - Jim Tucker, M. D.
8. *Between Two Worlds* - Tyler Henry
9. *Life After Death (Netflix TV Series)* - Tyler Henry
10. *Ghosts Among Us* - James van Praagh
11. *Zohar* - Kabbalah
12. *Super Attractor* - Gabby Bernstein
13. *Angels Among Us* - Kay Hilton/Julie Ryan
14. *Surviving Death (Netflix Season 1 Episode 6)* - Jim Tucker
15. *The Art Of Intuition* - Sophy Burnham
16. *Talking To Heaven* - James van Praagh
17. *Ask Julie Ryan Podcast* - Julie Ryan
18. *Embraced By The Light* - Betty J. Eadie
19. *What The Dead Have Taught Me About Living Well* - Rebecca Rosen
20. *Spirited* - Rebecca Rosen
21. *Saved By The Light* - Dannion Brinkley
22. *Secrets Of The Light* - Dannion Brinkley
23. *At Peace In The Lights* - Dannion Brinkley
24. *The Scientific And Spiritual Implications Of Psychic Abilities* - R. Targ, J. Katra - Research Paper
25. *Quantum Astrology* - Rick Levine
26. *The Astrology Podcast* - Chris Brennan

27. *Changing of the Gods* - Kenny Ausubel & Louie Schwartzberg
28. *Cosmos & Psyche* - Richard Tarnas
29. *Healing Grief* - James van Praagh
30. *Map of Heaven* - Eben Alexander, MD
31. *After life: Answers From The Other Side* - John Edward
32. *15 Ways To Increase Your Vibrations* - Terri Booth
33. *The Easy Part of the Hard Problem: A Resonance Theory of Consciousness* - Tam Hunt & Jonathan W. Schooler
34. *Healing Your Body* - Louis Hay
35. *Science And Religion* - Albert Einstein
36. *The Human Energy Field and the Invisible Universe* - Dr. Harry Oldfield
37. *Beginning Mediumship Workbook: How To Develop Your Mediumship Skills* - Carole Anne
38. *The Anastasi System - Psychic Development Level 1* - Sandy Anastasi
39. *Developing Your Own Psychic Powers* - John Edward
40. *Remote Viewing Exercises* - www.remoteviewed.com
41. *The Afterlife Unveiled* - Stafford Betty
42. *Heaven and Hell Unveiled: Updates from the World of Spirit* - Stafford Betty
43. *Life Between Heaven And Earth* - George Anderson & Andrew Barone
44. *Medical Medium - Celery Juice* - Anthony William
45. *Medical Medium* - Anthony William
46. *Anatomy of the Soul* - Carolyn Myss
47. *Advanced Energy Anatomy* - Carolyn Myss
48. *Mysticism: A Study of the Nature and Development of Man's Spiritual Consciousness* - Evelyn Underhill
49. *Psychic, Healers & Mediums* - Jennifer Weigel
50. *Life In The World Unseen* - Anthony Borgia
51. *Journey of Souls* - Michael Newton
52. *Destiny of Souls* - Michael Newton
53. *Life Between Lives* - Michael Newton
54. *The Human Energy Field And The Invisible Universe* - Harry Oldfield
55. *The Book of Mastery* - Paul Selig
56. *A Still, Small Voice: A Psychic's Guide To Awakening Intuition* - Echo Bodine
57. *The Afterlife of Leslie Stringfellow: A Nineteenth Century Family's Experience of Spiritualism* - Stephen Chism
58. *The Power of Love* - James van Praagh
59. *Money Master The Game* - Tony Robbins
60. *Walking In The Garden of Souls* - George Anderson

61. *Lessons From The Light* - George Anderson

62. *The Changing World Order* - Ray Dalio

63. *Application of Impossible Things* - Natalie Sudman

64. *Real Magic* - Dean Radin

65. *Super Attractor* - Gabrielle Bernstien

66. *The Practice of Tibetan Meditation* - Daisy Talk Rinpoche

67. *The Science of Getting Rich* - Wallace D. Wattles

68. *The Hard Work of Happiness* - Reb Buxton

69. *Happy Money* - Ken Honda

70. *A Still Small Voice* - Echo Bodine

71. *The Universal Christ* - Richard Rohr

72. *Chatter* - Ethan Kross

73. *Becoming Supernatural* - Dr. Joe Dispenza

74. *Golden* - Justin Zorn, Leigh Marz

75. *Teen Astrology - The Ultimate Guide To Making Your Life Your Own* - M. J. Abadie

76. *Outlive* - Peter Attia, MD

77. *The Book Of Five Rings* - Miyamoto Musashi

ABOUT THE AUTHOR

For twenty years, Reb worked as a psychotherapist. Over those two decades, he served as a case manager, center director, counselor, and in his own private practice. Reb founded *The Sacred Life,* an organization dedicated to helping men lead with love, wisdom, and integrity where he teaches *The Transformational Path*tm.

Reb is also the Founder & CEO of RiiGHT.ONE and SACRED.DATING. RiiGHT.ONE is a technology-based company improving how clients and therapists find one another. SACRED.DATING reimagines dating by making love, wisdom, and integrity the center of romantic relationships.

For more information, please visit: www.sacredlife.co, www.riight.one, and www.sacred.dating.

ENDNOTES

1. https://fortune.com/2023/01/12/fortune-500-companies-ceos-women-10-percent/
2. https://www.cnn.com/videos/us/2023/02/25/smr-young-men-in-trouble.cnn
3. https://thehill.com/blogs/blog-briefing-room/3868557-most-young-men-are-single-most-young-women-are-not/
4. https://www.cnn.com/2023/06/19/health/loneliness-social-isolation-early-death-risk-wellness/index.html
5. 1 Corinthians 13 1-2, 6-7 - The Message
6. https://www.youtube.com/watch?v=C6o0amydcLU
7. https://www.space.com/33553-biggest-thing-universe.html
8. For more information go to https://www.heartmath.org/research/science-of-the-heart/#
9. To see a map of neurons in the heart visit https://research.jefferson.edu/2022-magazine/the-hearts-little-brain.html
10. https://www.theguardian.com/science/2021/aug/15/the-hidden-sense-shaping-your-wellbeing-interoception
11. As referenced in https://www.heartmath.org/research/science-of-the-heart/#
12. www.sacredlife.co/muse
13. www.sacredlife.co/resources
14. https://www.ncbi.nlm.nih.gov/pmc/articles/PMC3060589/pdf/tjp0589-1095.pdf
15. https://www.healthonecares.com/healthy-living/blog/the-connection-between-your-smile-and-a-healthy-heart
16. www.sacredlife.co/three
17. https://www.bmj.com/content/323/7327/1450
18. Phillipians 4:6-7 - The Message
19. https://youtu.be/1Og42r5s3bE
20. Find an example of the Q.A.N. method at www.sacredlife.co/qan
21. www.sacredlife.co/spotify

22. www.sacredlife.co/powergrid
23. To see this photo visit www.sacredlife.co/mountain
24. www.sacredlife.co/transformation
25. Proverbs 21:23 - The Message
26. Romans 12:21 - Good News Bible
27. Pennebaker, James W. "Writing About Emotional Experiences as a Thera-peutic Process. 8, 3: 162–166." (1997)
28. Proverbs 4:23 - The Message
29. Mueller, C. M., and Dweck, C. S. (1998). Praise for intelligence can under-mine children's motivation and performance. J. Pers.Soc. Psychol. 75, 33–52. doi: 10.1037/0022-3514.75.1.33
30. https://www.windbridge.org/research
31. Matthew 7:17 - The Message
32. 1 John 4:18 - Good News Bible
33. www.sacredlife.co/rebel